Berlin 1945

End of the Thousand Year Reich

Campaign • 159

Berlin 1945

End of the Thousand Year Reich

Peter Antill • Illustrated by Peter Dennis

Series editor Lee Johnson

First published in Great Britain in 2005 by Osprey Publishing,
Midland House, West Way, Botley, Oxford OX2 0PH, United Kindgom.
443 Park Avenue South, New York, NY 10016, USA
Email: info@ospreypublishing.com

A CIP catalogue record for this book is available from the British Library

ISBN 1 84176 915 0

The author, Peter Antill, has asserted his right under the Copyright, Designs and
Patents Act, 1988, to be identified as the Author of this Work.

Design: The Black Spot
Index: Sandra Shotter
Maps by: The Map Studio
3d bird's-eye views by The Black Spot
Battlescene artwork by: Peter Dennis
Originated by PPS-Grasmere, Leeds, UK
Printed and bound in China through Worldprint

06 07 08 09 10   11 10 9 8 7 6 5 4 3 2

For a catalogue of all books published by Osprey please contact·

NORTH AMERICA
Osprey Direct, C/O Random House Distribution Center, 400 Hahn Road,
Westminster, MD 21157, USA
E-mail: info@ospreydirect.com

ALL OTHER REGIONS
Osprey Direct UK, P.O. Box 140, Wellingborough, Northants, NN8 2FA, UK
E-mail: info@ospreydirect.co.uk

www.ospreypublishing.com

Front cover image courtesy of Topfoto/Novosti

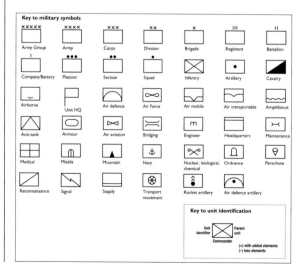

Author's Note

Two small points came to light during the research for this
book. The first is that I had to rely on modern cartography
to create the 2D maps and bird's eye views for the book
and many towns and villages that were still in German
territory during the events depicted are now in Poland, and
have been re-named. Therefore certain guesses had to be
made as to which German name corresponded to which
modern Polish town or village. The second is the
differences of opinion in many of the published books,
articles, manuscripts and online sources that I consulted.
Where the facts were not clear, I have taken an informed
view based on the available evidence.

Author's Acknowledgement

I would like to thank Louise Clarke and everyone at
TopFoto, Nik Cornish and Stavka, as well as Yvonne Oliver
and the staff of the Photographic Department of the
Imperial War Museum for allowing me to use the
photographs reproduced in this publication. A big thank
you goes to Alexander Stilwell, Peter Dennis and everyone
at Osprey for their patience and encouragement during this,
my second book for them, which happened to coincide
with my return to full-time education for a year. A final
thank you goes to my wife, Michelle, my parents, David
and Carole, and my parents-in-law, Sally and Alan, for
their patience, encouragement and enthusiasm.

CONTENTS

FROM THE VISTULA TO THE ODER, SOVIET OFFENSIVE OPERATIONS JAN–FEB 1945

1. The main Soviet attack began at 10.30 after a one-hour bombardment with two waves of tanks and three waves of infantry. Koniev committed some 34 infantry divisions and around 1,000 tanks to the first echelon (03.00, 12 January 1945).
2. Koniev then launched the 3rd and 4th Guards Tank Armies in a northeasterly direction to cut off the German forces retreating from Radom.
3. The 5th Guards Army advanced towards Czestochowa.
4. Rokossovsky attacked northwest towards Danzig in an attempt to cut off Army Group Centre. The Germans had little chance to respond as they were already under pressure from the 1st Baltic and 3rd Byelorussian Fronts.
5. Zhukov launched his attack on 14 January 1945, pushing rapidly out of the bridgehead at Magnuszew with the 5th Shock and 8th Guards Armies.
6. Zhukov's 33rd and 69th Armies broke out from the Pulawy bridgehead.
7. Zhukov sent the 1st Guards Tank Army off on an axis of advance incorporating Lódź and Poznan.
8. The 2nd Guards Tank Army drove forward with Plock and Incwroclaw in its axis of advance.
9. Koniev's forces reached the Warta River on 17 January 1945.
10. Warsaw fell on 17 January 1945.
11. The German 2nd Army collapsed, forcing the Gross Deutschland and XXIV Panzer Corps to withdraw, allowing Rokossovsky to complete the occupation of East Prussia and the encirclement of Danzig.
12. By early February, around 500,000 troops had been surrounded around Danzig and Königsberg but most of these, as well as troops from the Courland Peninsula, were evacuated in an operation masterminded by Admiral Karl Dönitz.
13. Gross Deutschland and XXIV Panzer Corps were then transferred to Army Group A (which later became Centre) arriving at Lódź just as the Soviets reached the city. They hurriedly withdrew through advancing Soviet columns to reach the Oder.
14. Zhukov reached the Oder by the beginning of February and, along with Koniev, consolidated along the river.
15. Poznan surrendered 23 February 1945.
16. Breslau was surrounded but held out until May.
17. The cruise liner *Willhelm Gustloff* was sunk by Soviet submarine S-13 off Stolpebank with the greatest recorded loss of life in a ship sinking – over 7,000 (23.08, 30 January 1945).

N

0	50 miles
0	100km

Front line 12 January 1945
Front line 24 February 1945
Soviet attacks
German withdrawals
Isolated German positions mid-March
German bypassed positions and fortress cities

INTRODUCTION

The Battle for Berlin in April–May 1945 may not have been the final battle of the Second World War in Europe, but it was certainly the concluding one. Directive No. 21 issued on 18 December 1940, tasked the Wehrmacht with crushing the Soviet Union, even before the war with Britain had been concluded. Therefore, on 22 June 1941, Germany invaded the Soviet Union with a force of over 3 million men in 152 divisions, along with over 30 divisions from her allies. This surprise attack was meant to destroy the Red Army in one swift campaign and, in so doing, indirectly force Britain to the negotiating table before the United States could enter the war. Hitler, however, had both overestimated the capability of the Wehrmacht to deliver such a crushing blow over such a short period of time, and underestimated the capacity of the Soviet Union to survive it and mobilize its human, industrial and technological resources to resist the invasion.

Just under four years later, the Soviet assault on Berlin was the culmination of a remorseless effort by the Soviet Union to push the Germans out of the USSR and then westwards out of Eastern Europe, having wrested the strategic initiative from the Germans after Operation *Zitadelle*, the Battle of Kursk, in July 1943. By August 1944 the Red Army had reached the outskirts of Warsaw, having decimated Army Group Centre in Operation *Bagration* in June and captured Bucharest on 31 August. However, they were unable to lend any assistance to the Polish Home Army as it rose against the Germans on 1 August 1944. There were four Panzer divisions between the Red Army and the Polish insurgents in Warsaw and Rokossovsky's forces desperately needed time to regroup after

Soviet soldiers preparing a piece of heavy artillery. The Soviets placed a great deal of emphasis on the use of large concentrations of artillery in preparation for an attack. The numbers of guns per metre of front were some of the highest ever seen in the Berlin operation. (From the fonds of the RGAKFD at Krasnogorsk)

the summer offensive. The result was that, despite the Soviets dropping supplies to the insurgents towards the end of September, the Home Army had been crushed by overwhelming German force by 2 October. The rest of the year saw the Red Army reoccupying the Baltic States, with the exception of the Courland Peninsula, which contained Army Group North with the 16th and 18th Armies and the area around Memel that was held by the XXVIII Corps. The Red Army also advanced into Bulgaria and Hungary, reaching the outskirts of Budapest by the end of October.

The Soviet offensive was to re-start on 20 January 1945, but due to the German offensive in the Ardennes and a request from Churchill to Stalin to bring forward the Red Army's offensive to take the pressure off the Western Allies, Stalin ordered that it be brought forward to 12 January 1945. The Soviet High Command (also known as Stavka) had prepared two offensives, separated geographically by the course of the River Vistula. The first, and the stronger of the two, would see the 1st Byelorussian Front under Zhukov break out of the Pulawy bridgehead towards Lodz, out of the Magnuszew bridgehead towards Kutno and encircle Warsaw. The 1st Ukrainian Front, under Marshal Ivan S. Koniev, would advance from the Baranow bridgehead towards Radom and send a force northwest to encircle the German forces trying to retreat from the Radom area, collaborating with 1st Byelorussian as necessary. They would be assisted in their breakout by the 4th Ukrainian Front on their left, and after the breakout had been accomplished, advance west and northwest towards the Oder. The second offensive was to be undertaken by Marshal Konstantin K. Rokossovsky's 2nd Byelorussian Front that would break out of the Rozan and Serock bridgeheads, striking northwest to reach the Baltic coast, cut off East Prussia and clear the lower Vistula. On his right, 3rd Byelorussian Front under Gen Ivan D. Chernyakhovskii, was to attack in a westerly direction south of the Pregel River towards Königsberg, splitting the 3rd Panzer Army off from the

An abandoned T-34/76 that has come to grief in the soft ground of the Oder River valley. The difficult going and determined German defence slowed the advance of the 1st Byelorussian Front to the extent that Zhukov was forced to commit his two tank armies early. (Nik Cornish Library)

Soviet infantry advance at a run while being covered by their comrades. Despite the enormous numbers of tanks being fielded by the Red Army, infantry were still an essential part of the combined arms team, particularly in urban fighting. (From the fonds of the RGAKFD at Krasnogorsk)

rest of Army Group Centre and envelop the 4th Army around the Masurian Lakes.

Between September and January the Soviet High Command gave massive logistical support to the preparations for the coming offensive. The railways in eastern Poland were converted to the narrow Russian gauge and 1st Byelorussian Front received over 68,000 carloads of supplies, not far off the amount received by all four fronts in Operation *Bagration*, while over 64,000 carloads of supplies went to 1st Ukrainian Front. The 1st Byelorussian Front stockpiled some 1.3 million artillery shells at the Pulawy bridgehead and 2.5 million at the Magnuszew bridgehead. The 2nd and 3rd Byelorussian fronts would have a combined artillery and mortar stockpile of around 9 million rounds. By comparison, the Don Front had fired under a million shells during the entire Stalingrad operation. The Soviet High Command also changed its troop indoctrination programme. For almost 18 months, the central theme had been the liberation of Soviet territory but Soviet forces would soon be fighting on foreign soil and so the new theme would be vengeance. It was disseminated by posters, slogans, meetings, lectures, signposts, articles and leaflets. Political officers recounted tales of crimes that German troops had committed (real or imagined) against Russian civilians and the looting and destruction carried out across the country. Unfortunately, such methods eventually proved counter-productive as the conduct of Soviet troops soon became such that it was of grave concern to the Political Department and when German troops re-took an East Prussian village after Soviet occupation, they found it completely empty with its inhabitants massacred. Göbbels was able to use the propaganda value of this incident to the full and ensured that the Soviets would face stiff, even fanatical resistance from German troops for the remainder of the war.

The Soviet offensive started at 0500hrs on 12 January 1945 when Koniev opened with an intense artillery barrage followed closely by reconnaissance and penal battalions. They took the first line of trenches and paused while the artillery struck the second. It also disrupted the 4th Panzer Army's Command Post and the mobile reserves that had

been positioned too close to the main line. By the early afternoon, huge gaps had been torn in the German first line and elements of the 4th Guards Tank Army sent in to exploit them. By the evening, the Soviets had penetrated the German defences to a depth of 20 miles across a 25-mile stretch of front. Over the next couple of days, Kielce fell, securing Koniev's right flank, and his armies spread out into open country towards Kraków, Kantowice and Czestochowa, the Germans withdrawing to avoid encirclement. The Gross Deutschland and XXIV Panzer Corps were sent to stiffen the defences of Kielce but as they arrived in Lodz they were confronted by advancing Soviet forces and had to withdraw in haste.

Zhukov attacked on 14 January out of the Magnuszew bridgehead and managed to achieve tactical surprise with the forward assault battalions, with which he relentlessly followed up by quickly committing his main assault force and the leading elements of the 2nd Guards Tank Army. The 5th Shock, 8th Guards and 1st Guards Tank Armies went into action soon after that, with the 47th and 61st Armies moving to encircle Warsaw, which the Germans hastily evacuated. The fall of Warsaw bought bitter recrimination from Hitler who removed Harpe from Army Group A and replaced him with Schörner and dismissed von Lüttwitz from the 9th Army and replaced him with Busse. Added to this, he pulled the 6th SS Panzer Army away from the Ardennes and instead of putting it into the line in Poland to try and stem the Soviet tide, sent it to recapture Hungary.

By 20 January, the Soviets had broken through along a 350-mile front and had taken Kraków and Lodz. Zhukov's 33rd Army managed to locate Koniev's right flank near Ilza while the remainder of 1st Byelorussian headed northwest with the German frontier only some 40 miles away. The honour of being first to cross it, though, went to Koniev, whose main

A Soviet T-34/76, accompanied by an infantry detachment, crosses a road behind a knocked out Tiger I. It is unlikely that a single T-34/76 could have accomplished this feat without the aid of several compatriots, probably T-34/85s or Josef Stalin II tanks. (From the fonds of the RGAKFD at Krasnogorsk)

armoured thrust was now directed towards Breslau under Stavka's instructions. Koniev then directed a substantial part of his forces to take the Silesian industrial region. Meanwhile, Zhukov continued to press towards Küstrin on the Oder but was aware that a gap was opening up in his right flank between his front and the 2nd Byelorussian under Rokossovsky who was advancing almost northwards to cut off the German forces in East Prussia. Zhukov redeployed the 3rd Shock, 47th and 61st Armies to cover his flank. Rokossovsky's attack on 14 January had initially run into determined resistance along with counterattacks from the Gross Deutschland Panzer Corps but, with that formation's transfer south, Rokossovsky committed strong tank elements alongside the 48th, 2nd Shock and 65th Armies, breaking through along a 60-mile front on 19 January. To his right was Chernyakovskii's 3rd Byelorussian Front, which was to cooperate with Rokossovsky in eliminating the German forces in East Prussia. They found that they faced the strongest part of the German defence and had to literally batter their way through, sustaining heavy casualties as a result. Eventually, Stavka transferred reinforcements in the form of 43rd Army from the 1st Baltic Front to the 3rd Byelorussian Front. Marienburg and Elbing fell on 26 January, cutting off Königsberg, as well as the German 3rd Panzer Army, 4th Army and elements of 2nd Army. Despite a powerful breakout attempt by 4th Army (involving eight divisions – six infantry, one motorized and one Panzer) that commenced on 27 January 1945, the German forces remained trapped in East Prussia. By early February, both Koniev and Zhukov had reached the Oder and were consolidating their gains. Rokossovsky, Chernyakovskii (who was killed on 18 February and replaced by Marshal Alexandr M. Vasilevskii) and Bagramyan kept up the pressure on the remaining pockets of German resistance, including Königsberg, Memel, Bromberg, Poznan and Breslau, with Rokossovsky occupying East Pomerania during the remainder of the month. The stage was set, therefore, for the final Soviet offensive aimed at capturing the capital of Nazi Germany and the heart of the Third Reich – Berlin.

CHRONOLOGY

1939

28 August Nazi-Soviet Non-Aggression Pact is signed in Moscow.
1 September Germany invades Poland.
3 September Britain and France declare war on Germany.
17 September The Soviet Union occupies its share of territory as outlined in the Nazi-Soviet Pact, including eastern Poland and the Baltic States.

1940

25 August First RAF raid over Berlin.

1941

22 June Germany launches Operation *Barbarossa*, the most ambitious campaign of the Second World War, to defeat the Soviet Union.

1942

12 May First contingent of the US Eighth Air Force arrives in Britain.

1943

2 February The last German forces in Stalingrad surrender.
5 July Germany begins Operation *Zitadelle*.
6 August Berlin is partially evacuated to lessen the impact of bombing raids.
18 November RAF starts its 'Battle of Berlin'.

1944

6 March First major USAAF raid on Berlin.
23 June The Soviets begin Operation *Bagration*, which decisively defeats Army Group Centre.

1945

12 January The Red Army begins its winter offensive involving the 1st, 2nd and 3rd Byelorussian and 1st Ukrainian Fronts.
16 January Hitler returns to Berlin.
27 January The Soviets liberate the camp at Auschwitz.
31 January Zhukov reaches the Oder.
4 February The Yalta conference begins.
11 February The Soviets capture Budapest.
21 March Heinrici appointed to command Army Group Vistula.
23 March 2nd Byelorussian Front begins final assault on Danzig.
30 March Danzig falls.
1 April Stavka meeting in Moscow between Zhukov, Koniev and Stalin.
9 April Red Army finally takes Königsberg after a 59-day siege.
10 April US 9th Army takes Essen and Hannover.
13 April Soviet forces capture Vienna.

A Soviet machinegun and crew in the suburbs of Berlin. As the Soviets advanced into Berlin, the burden of the fighting fell more and more on the infantry with armour and artillery playing a supporting role. (From the fonds of the RGAKFD at Krasnogorsk)

15 April British troops liberate Belsen.

16 April Soviets launch Operation *Berlin*.

18/19 April Last RAF air raid on Berlin.

19 April British 2nd Army reaches Lauenburg on the Elbe River. Zhukov breaks through the German defence lines on the Seelow Heights.

20 April 2nd Byelorussian Front begins its offensive across the lower Vistula.

24 April Elements of the German 9th Army are surrounded southeast of Berlin. Soviet forces reach the transmitter station at Nauen some 20 miles west of Berlin.

25 April The encirclement of Berlin is complete. US 1st Army and Soviet 5th Guards Army link up near Torgau.

26 April The German 12th Army begins its counterattack towards Berlin. The 2nd Byelorussian Front takes Stettin.

29 April Hitler marries Eva Braun and prepares his last will and testament. The Kremlin announces a provisional government for Austria without consulting the Western Allies.

30 April Hitler and Eva Braun commit suicide at around 15.20. Soviets assault the Reichstag, raising the Red Flag at 22.50.

1 May Dönitz broadcasts news of Hitler's death. Göbbels and his wife commit suicide after killing their six children.

2 May Soviet troops storm the Reichs Chancellery. Berlin Garrison surrenders on the orders of General Weidling.

4 May German forces in northwest Germany, Netherlands and Denmark surrender to Field Marshal Montgomery.

6 May Soviet offensive begins against Army Group Centre. Breslau surrenders.

7 May Jodl signs the surrender documents at SHAEF headquarters at Rheims.

8 May VE Day in Western Europe and USA. Keitel, Stumpff and von Friedeburg sign the surrender documents in Berlin at Marshal Zhukov's headquarters.

1 July US forces enter Berlin. The British arrive the next day.

17 July Potsdam conference begins.

1947

18 July The seven prisoners convicted of War Crimes at the Nuremberg Trials arrive to begin their sentences at Spandau Prison.

1948

24 June Soviets cut all road and rail communications between West Germany and Berlin forcing the Western Allies to undertake an airlift to supply the city.

1953

17 June Popular strikes and demonstrations occur in Berlin and all over the GDR at the proposal by the East German Government to increase production targets without increasing wages.

1961

12 August The GDR begins construction of the Berlin Wall.

1962

17 August Eighteen-year-old Peter Fechter is shot while trying to escape over the wall and left to bleed to death in front of hundreds of horrified West Berliners and journalists.

1963

26 June President John F. Kennedy's speech outside the Schöneberg Town Hall.

1971

3 September Quadripartite Agreement signed between the Four Powers in Berlin.

1989

9 November The Berlin Wall is opened for the first time and thousands of East Berliners surge through to the West.

1990

3 October The unification of the Federal Republic and GDR occurs.

1991

20 June The Bundestag takes the decision that Berlin will become the capital of the newly unified Germany.

1999

19 April After a four-year renovation, led by the British architect Sir Norman Foster, the Federal German Bundestag holds its first debate in the Reichstag.

OPPOSING COMMANDERS

Marshal Georgi Zhukov, shown signing the Joint Declaration of the Allied Commanders-in-Chief, relating to Berlin and its division into four zones of occupation, 5 June 1945. Stalin was always concerned over Zhukov's popularity and always sought a way of keeping him in check. He even had a former chief of staff questioned. (Topfoto)

SOVIET COMMANDERS

The two main formations involved in Operation *Berlin* were the 1st Byelorussian Front under **Marshal Georgi K. Zhukov** (1896–1974) and the 1st Ukrainian Front under Marshal Koniev. Zhukov, the son of a village cobbler, was conscripted into the Imperial Russian Army in 1915 but joined the Red Army in 1918 and the Communist Party in 1919. By 1938 he had risen to the post of Deputy Commander, Byelorussian Military District and was sent to repel the Japanese incursion into Mongolia. He was then promoted to full General and given the command of the Kiev Special Military District, followed by Chief of the General Staff and a Deputy Minister of Defence. Given command of the Leningrad Front, he stopped the German advance at the gates of the city, after which he coordinated the defence of Moscow, the Battle for Stalingrad and the Battle for Kursk. He was promoted to a Marshal of the Soviet Union in 1943, commanded the 1st Ukrainian Front in early 1944 and led Operation *Bagration* in June. After the war he remained as Commander, Group of Soviet Forces Germany until March 1946 and commanded the Odessa and Ural Military Districts after a short period as a Deputy Minister of Defence. It is rumoured that Zhukov (along with Koniev) played a role in the arrest of Lavrentii Beria (Head of the NKVD) and supported Krushchev during his attempted removal in June 1957.

Marshal Ivan S. Koniev (1897–1973) fought in the First World War as well and joined the Communist Party in 1918. He received officer training at the Frunze Military Academy during the mid-1920s and barely escaped with his life during Stalin's purges of the 1930s. After commanding the Western Front, during the defence of Moscow, he was placed in command of the Steppe Military District in June 1943, which became the Steppe Front in July. He won renown for his crushing of the Korsun Pocket, the dramatic 'liberation' of the Ukraine and southern Poland, and was instrumental in both the operation to capture Berlin and to occupy Czechoslovakia. After the war, Koniev was appointed as Military Governor of the Soviet occupation zone in Austria, commanded the military forces set up as part of the Warsaw Treaty Organization (Warsaw Pact) as well as the Group of Soviet Forces Germany.

On the immediate flanks of these two formations were the 2nd Byelorussian and 4th Ukrainian Fronts. The 2nd Byelorussian was under the command of **Marshal Konstantin K. Rokossovsky** (1896–1968), a former Tsarist cavalry NCO who joined the Red Army in 1918.

He was imprisoned during the purges but released in March 1940 after the Russo-Finnish War on the orders of Stalin himself. He was seriously wounded during the fighting around Moscow, but returned to

duty in September 1942 just in time to take part in the Battle for Stalingrad. He commanded the Central Front during the Battle for Kursk and then went on to command a number of fronts until the end of the war. After the war he went on to hold the posts of Deputy Minister of Defence and Inspector General of the Ministry of Defence, and returned to Poland (he was Polish by birth) as Minister of National Defence between 1949 and 1956.

Colonel-General Andrei I. Yeremenko (1892–1970) replaced ColGen I.E. Petrov as commander of the 4th Ukrainian Front at the end of March 1945. He fought during both the First World War and the Russian Civil War and graduated from the Frunze Military Academy in 1935. Yeremenko commanded the 6th Cavalry Corps during the invasion and partition of Poland and by 1941 he was commanding the Transbaikal Military District, but was recalled by Stalin after the Germans invaded and given command of firstly, the Western Front and then the Bryansk Front. He led a counterattack which stalled the German drive on Moscow, thus helping to save the city, and contributed to the defence of Stalingrad as commander of the Southeastern Front (which was renamed Stalingrad Front, then Southern Front). Command of various formations followed as did action in the Caucasus, Crimea, the Baltic and Hungary, but in May 1945 his 4th Ukrainian Front surrounded Army Group Centre in conjunction with Koniev's forces.

Colonel-General Vassilli I. Chuikov (1900–1982) commanded the 8th Guards Army during the assault on Berlin. He had joined the Red Army in 1919 and rose through the ranks quickly, mainly due to his membership of the Communist Party. He attended the Frunze Military Academy, took part in the Soviet occupation of eastern Poland and the Russo-Finnish War and served as a military adviser to Chiang Kai-shek. In May 1942 he was recalled and placed in command of the 62nd Army, which defended Stalingrad against the German 6th Army. He was then promoted to command the 8th Guards Army, which he commanded for the rest of the war. After the war he served as Commander, Group of

RIGHT **A photo showing Gen A. I. Yeremenko at a forward field command post, directing operations. He commanded a number of formations, including the 2nd Baltic Front but took over the 4th Ukrainian Front from Gen Petrov in March 1945 and cooperated with Koniev's 1st Ukrainian Front to surround Army Group Centre in Czechoslovakia. (Topfoto)**

ABOVE **Gen Vassilli Chuikov commanded the 8th Guards Army during Operation** *Berlin*. **He was joined by Katukov's 1st Guards Tank Army after the costly breakthrough on the Seelow Heights had caused serious casualties to both formations. After that, Zhukov had them fight together for the rest of the battle. (Topfoto/Topham)**

Soviet Forces Germany from 1949 until 1953, commanded the Kiev Military District and, after having been made a Marshal of the Soviet Union in 1955, was appointed Commander-in-Chief of the Soviet Ground Forces in 1960.

In command of the 1st Guards Tank Army was **Colonel-General Mikhail Y. Katukov** (1900–1976). Katukov joined the Red Army in 1919 and gradually worked his way through the ranks, finally being promoted to Captain in July 1936 after having attended the Stalin Military Academy the previous year. His first major command came in October 1938 when he was appointed Acting Commanding Officer, 5th Light Tank Brigade, 45th Mechanized Corps. From there he went on to command the 20th Tank Division and with the onset of war, took command of the 4th Tank Brigade, 1st Tank Corps, 4th Tank Corps and finally the 1st Guards Tank Army in January 1943, a post he held until the end of the Second World War. After the war he attended the Voroshilov Military Academy in 1951 and was made Inspector General of Tanks (1955). This was followed by the post of Inspector General of Army Tank Divisions in 1957 and two senior posts in the Ministry of Defence.

Colonel-General Vasily I. Kutznetsov (1894–1964), was commander of 3rd Shock Army, which finally took the Reichstag after a bitter campaign. He had fought to defend Kiev in 1941 and had been blamed for the disaster which befell the Red Army, deflecting attention away from Marshal Budenny. After a period of disgrace, he returned to the front line with the command of the 1st Guards Army at the Battle for Stalingrad and was assigned as the Deputy Commander of the Southwest Front between 1942 and 1943. He was critical of the 1st Byelorussian Front's plan of attack and, after the offensive had ground to a halt, commented to General Popiel that it had been due to the fact that the Germans had been well prepared to counter Soviet methods.

Colonel F. M. Zinchenko was the commander of the 756th Rifle Regiment (150th Rifle Division), one of the regiments that fought for **17**

control of the Reichstag. It was Sergeants M. A. Yegorov and M. V. Kantaria, in a party led by Lt Berest from the 1st Battalion under Capt Stefan A. Neustroyev, who finally planted the Red Flag on the roof at 22.50. The famous photograph taken by Ukrainian war photographer Yevgeny Khaldei was actually a re-enactment, staged sometime later.

GERMAN COMMANDERS

General der Artillerie Helmuth Weidling was the commander of LVI Panzer Corps, originally part of the 9th Army under Gen Theodor Busse, helping to defend the Seelow Heights. When the 1st Byelorussian Front finally broke through, the Corps retreated directly back to Berlin, where, against Weidling's better judgement, it substantially stiffened the city's defences. Weidling took over the command of the Berlin Defence Area on 23 April 1945, moving his headquarters into the Bendler Block. Weidling had fought with the Imperial German Army during the First World War and manned airships on tactical missions, for which they were awarded a unique badge consisting of an airship on top of a laurel wreath, a decoration he shared with GenLt Fritz Koreuber. He had also commanded the 86th Infantry Division at Kursk and the XLI Panzer Corps during the withdrawal through Byelorussia into East Prussia.

SS-Brigadeführer Wilhelm Mohnke commanded the 'Central Government Area' within the 'Zitadelle' (the nickname for the Inner Defence Area of Berlin) that included the Reichs Chancellery, Führerbunker and Reichstag. Born in 1911 in Lübeck, Mohnke joined the NSDAP (Nazi Party) in September 1931, becoming one of the original members of the SS-Stabswach Berlin (Chancellery Guard). Mohnke gradually rose through the ranks, commanding the 2nd Battalion of the Leibstandarte Adolf Hitler during the 1940 campaign; the 26th SS Panzergrenadier Regiment of the 12th SS 'Hitlerjugend' Panzer Division in Normandy and the 1st SS 'Leibstandarte Adolf Hitler' Panzer Division during the Ardennes Offensive. It was while in these particular posts that troops under his command were accused of committing a number of atrocities against enemy PoWs. These included the murder of 80 British PoWs at Wormhout in May 1940, the killing of 35 Canadian PoWs at Fountenay le Pesnel during the Battle for Normandy and the massacre of 84 American PoWs in December 1944 near Malmedy. Mohnke was captured during his attempted breakout from the Führerbunker and spent ten years as a prisoner before being released in 1955.

In command of Army Group Centre was the newly promoted **Generalfeldmarschall Ferdinand Schörner** (1892–1973) who joined the Bavarian Leib Infantry Regiment and saw action in the First World War, fighting at Verdun and the Isonzo River, where he was awarded the Pour Le Merite (Blue Max). After the war he became involved in right-wing politics and joined the Reichswehr. After joining the 19th Bavarian Infantry Regiment, he was sent to the Dresden Infantry School, managing to obtain a number of General Staff postings before gaining command of the 98th Gebirgsjäger Regiment in 1937 and being promoted to Oberstleutnant. Schörner was next given command of 6th Gebirgs Division, which he led during the Balkan Campaign and then on the Eastern Front in the north

Col F. M. Zinchenko (pointing), whose 756th Rifle Regiment took part in the storming of the Reichstag, reports to Gen Vassily Kutznetsov (third from left, second row of officers). Kutznetsov was commander of the 3rd Shock Army and critical of the way the attack on the Seelow Heights was conducted. (Topfoto/Topham)

SS-Brigaf Wilhelm Mohnke, commander of the Central Government District including the Reichs Chancellery, Reichstag and the Führerbunker. Tensions between the Wehrmacht and the Waffen SS persisted right through the war, where even during the battle for Berlin, Mohnke reported directly to Hitler, ignoring the garrison chain of command through 'Zitadelle' to Weidling. (Topfoto/Topham)

ABOVE **GenObst Gotthard Heinrici, an outstanding Panzer commander, commanded Army Group Vistula after Himmler had been relieved of its command. He refused to follow the Führer's instructions to defend Berlin at all costs having realized the war was over and covertly worked to get as many soldiers and civilians to the west as possible. (Topfoto)**

ABOVE, RIGHT **Gen der Panzertruppen Walther Wenck was a naturally gifted staff officer. He took control of the 12th Army in April 1945 and not only turned his army around from its Elbe positions where it faced the US Army but attacked towards Berlin, reaching the outskirts of Berlin and linking up with the 9th Army. (Topfoto)**

of Finland. Command of the 19th Corps and XL Panzer Corps followed. In March 1944 he was promoted to Generaloberst and made commander of Army Group Ukraine. In January 1945, Schörner became commander of the new Army Group Centre, which conducted a fighting retreat westwards, enabling over one-and-a-half million people from Eastern Germany to escape the Red Army.

Generaloberst Gotthard Heinrici (1886–1971), an outstanding Panzer commander, particularly in defensive operations, he commanded Army Group Vistula during the last phase of the war. He fought during the First World War on both the Western and Eastern Fronts, alternating between staff and frontline duties. He remained in the Army after the war and eventually became a Generalmajor in 1936. He commanded the XXII Corps during the blitzkrieg against the Low Countries and France in 1940 and served under Heinz Guderian in the 2nd Panzer Army during Operation *Barbarossa*. In January 1942 he was promoted to Generaloberst and commander of the 4th Army which he led, developing excellent defensive tactics against the Red Army for the next two years. In August 1944 he was appointed to the command of the 1st Panzer Army and in March 1945, Army Group Vistula. By now he had realized Berlin was indefensible and refused Hitler's instructions to defend the city at all costs and was dismissed by Keitel. Heinrici surrendered to British forces in Flensberg and remained as a PoW until May 1948.

General der Panzertruppen Baron Hasso von Manteuffel (1897–1978) had the unenviable task of commanding the 3rd Panzer Army, the formation in Heinrici's Army Group Vistula facing Rokossovsky's 2nd Byelorussian Front across the River Oder. Von Manteuffel was brash but had great courage and tactical skill, coming to the personal attention of the Führer. He had served as a cavalry officer during the First World War and afterwards decided to stay in the army, transferring to the new Panzer arm in 1934. He commanded an infantry battalion in Rommel's 7th Panzer Division, rising to command the 6th Panzer Grenadier Regiment during the opening phases of Operation *Barbarossa* where he earned the Knight's Cross. Having been promoted to Oberst, he then took command of the 7th Panzergrenadier Brigade in North Africa and commanded an improvised division during the battle for Tunisia. Command of the 7th Panzer Division and Grossdeutschland Panzergrenadier Division quickly followed (as did the Oakleaf Cluster) and in September 1944 was personally given command of the 5th Panzer Army that was to take part in the German counteroffensive in the Ardennes. Von Manteuffel was then transferred to the Eastern Front to command the 3rd Panzer Army, and was awarded the Swords and Diamonds to his Knight's Cross. He surrendered, along with the 3rd Panzer Army to the Western Allies on 3 May 1945.

General der Infanterie Theodor Busse (1897–1986) was born in Frankfurt an der Oder and joined the German Army as an officer cadet in 1915, being commissioned in February 1917. After the war, he joined the newly formed Reichswehr and, after the outbreak of the Second World War, held a number of staff positions between 1941 and 1944. He served as Chief of Staff to Generalfeldmarschall Erich von Manstein in Army Group South, as well as having posts as Chief of Staff in the 11th Army, Army Group Don and Army Group North Ukraine. On 30 January 1944 he was awarded the Knight's Cross and went on to take command of both the 121st Infantry Division and I Corps, before being appointed as the commander of the 9th Army to the east of Berlin in late January 1945. After the commencement of Operation *Berlin*, the 9th Army found itself surrounded along with thousands of refugees but Busse conspired with Wenck to break out and head west towards the American forces on the River Elbe. He spent some time as a PoW (1945–47) and after the war was the Director of Civil Defence in the West German Government and wrote a number of books on military history.

General der Panzertruppen Walther Wenck (1900–82) was appointed commander of the 12th Army on 10 April 1945. Born in Wittenberg, he was too young to serve in the First World War and so joined the Reichswehr. He enlisted in the infantry and caught the eye of, and became aide to, GenObst Hans von Seeckt. Wenck attended the Staff College and was promoted to Major and made the Operations Officer of 1st Panzer Division in which he served in both Poland and France. He proved to be a naturally gifted staff officer and was appointed as Chief of Staff of Gen Kirchner's LVII Corps. After that came a temporary assignment as Chief of Staff to the 3rd Rumanian Army under General Dumitrescu during the Battle for Stalingrad for which he was awarded the Knight's Cross. There followed a number of Chief of Staff posts to the 6th Army, 1st Panzer Army (that also saw a promotion to Generalmajor), Army Group South Ukraine and Director of Operations and Deputy Chief of Staff for OKH. He took over command of the 12th Army in April 1945. After the war, he spent two years in American captivity as a PoW and then joined a commercial firm, becoming Chairman of the Board of Directors in 1955.

Gen der Panzertruppen Hasso von Manteuffel who commanded the 3rd Panzer Army is shown here (on the far left) on 10 September 1951 at a hotel in Bonn. Von Manteuffel's forces faced the numerically superior 2nd Byelorussian Front but managed to hold it on the Oder for seven days. (Topfoto/Topham)

OPPOSING ARMIES

SOVIET FORCES

By the beginning of 1945, the Red Army possessed some six million troops on the Western Front, ranged against just over two million German and Axis troops. Rather than spread them evenly over the entire front (as the Germans were forced to do) they maintained a system of reserves under the control of the Soviet High Command that could distribute them according to where it wanted its main effort to be focused.

By this stage in the war, the Red Army was being sustained not only by the domestic industrial effort, much of it from the factories moved east to the Urals, but also by substantial quantities of American and British Lend-Lease material. This included soft-skinned vehicles, tanks, clothing and food, the latter being especially important as the traditional crop-growing areas of the USSR had been the very areas that had been occupied by the Axis and thus were in no state to support the vast numbers of troops now deployed in the field. However, Soviet industry was able to produce some 29,000 tanks and self-propelled guns, 122,500 artillery pieces and mortars, 40,300 aircraft and 184 million shells, mines and bombs in 1944 alone.

The soft-skinned vehicles provided the Red Army with the necessary mobility to transport not only troops and artillery pieces, but supplies and support equipment as well. One of the major advantages the Soviets had over the Germans was in engineering support and logistics. Forward combat units were often reinforced with specialist engineer battalions, due to the extensive use of fortifications and minefields by the Germans, which necessitated the deployment of mine-sweeping and flame-throwing tanks and combat engineer units. The standard German practice of destroying every bridge over streams and rivers as they retreated also necessitated the Red Army having substantial numbers of specialist engineer bridging units deployed forward. In addition, normal units were usually given special river-crossing and swamp-crossing training.

Infantry armies were divided into Guards, Shock and normal infantry armies. Guards armies were usually organized on a combined-arms basis with three infantry and one armoured corps, while the Shock armies would have greater artillery resources as they were designated as the assault formations that would have to breach the enemy defence system at the start of an offensive. The remaining infantry formations were often of a much lower calibre and while well equipped with light weapons, lacked the substantial artillery firepower of the Guards and Shock armies; what artillery they did have tended to be horse-drawn. They had the lowest priority on supplies (even food and clothing) and were almost expected to live off the land. Training tended to be minimal and, as a consequence, **21**

A Soviet Josef Stalin II tank with accompanying infantry crossing a river on the way to Berlin via an improvised pontoon bridge. In the close-quarters fighting in Berlin, even a powerful tank such as a JS II was vulnerable to German infantry anti-tank weapons. (From the fonds of the RGAKFD at Krasnogorsk)

morale and discipline suffered. Even so, discipline varied from unit to unit and the customary heavy bouts of drinking would inevitably lead to problems and acts of violence. However, the Soviet soldier usually had a good, close relationship with his officers, as the Red Army (and later the Soviet Army) relied on its officers to conduct the duties usually given to the NCOs in Western armies. This relationship was not readily extended to the political commissars who were regarded with distrust. Each army had from one to three NKVD (Ministry of the Interior) regiments attached, not as combat formations, but to act as a support service undertaking duties such as screening the rear of the parent formation, helping with traffic control and undertaking political indoctrination. Even worse off than these formations, however, were the penal units, each front having three battalions and each army from between five and ten companies. Officers were sent to the penal battalions and men to the penal companies, all as 'penal privates', where they could regain their rank and position by distinguished conduct in battle, after being killed in action or after recovering from wounds received and being returned to duty. These units were used for the most difficult and dangerous tasks, such as swamping enemy positions with sheer weight of numbers or advancing first over minefields to clear the way.

The Red Army enjoyed substantial superiority not only in manpower but also tanks and aircraft. By focusing on a small number of simple designs, the Soviets had produced some very good tanks; despite the fact they tended to have a much rougher finish than their German counterparts. The new JS-2 (Josef Stalin) 60-ton heavy tank mounted a 122mm gun and carried 28 rounds but the majority of Soviet tanks were medium tanks. These were mainly the 36-ton T-34/76, armed with a 76mm gun, but there were an increasing number of the later T-34/85, armed with an 85mm gun and carrying over 70 rounds. There was also the light T-70 tank armed with a 45mm gun, but that was mainly used to protect tactical headquarters in battle. The Guards armoured units were usually equipped with the JS-2 and T-34/85 but other formations usually had a mix of T-34 variants and Allied Lend-Lease equipment, the 2nd Guards Tank Army being a prime example, having American M4A2 Sherman tanks with 76mm guns and a few British Valentine tanks. The Red Army also made extensive use of tank destroyers, including the SU-85 and SU-100, based on the T-34 chassis. The SU-85s tended to be organised into battalions of 21 guns and the SU-100 organized into Guards brigades of 65 guns apiece. To support these formations, the Soviets had an effective system of vehicle recovery and repair through damaged-vehicle assembly points, where the workshops were able to put back into service around half the vehicles brought into them.

The most effective ground-attack aircraft the Soviets had was the IL-2 Shturmovik and air liaison units were posted to the headquarters of fronts, armies and forward brigades in order to improve the coordination with the ground forces. At this stage in the war, the Soviet Air Force outnumbered the Luftwaffe by over five-to-one and so could dominate the airspace over the battlefield.

The Soviets viewed the artillery arm as the 'King' of the battlefield and by the time of the drive on Berlin had amassed enough artillery to be able to concentrate a formidable amount of guns per kilometre on the axes of attack on which they were determined to achieve a breakthrough. The main artillery pieces used were the 76mm and 122mm towed guns but there were a number of independent artillery regiments equipped with larger calibre guns, such as a 152mm gun mounted in an open-tracked carriage and a 120mm heavy mortar. There were also self-propelled guns, the main models being the SU-76, SU-85, SU-100, JSU-122 and JSU-152, all carrying guns of the appropriate calibre, most of them fully enclosed and organized into independent regiments of the same vehicle. The SU-76 was in fact the most common and had originally been a tank destroyer based on the T-70 chassis carrying 60 rounds. Its open-topped superstructure meant that it was no longer suitable for that role and so was now deployed in a direct infantry support role, in battalions of four batteries with four guns each. The larger calibre 122mm and 152mm guns were deployed on both KV and JS tank chassis. The 122mm gun was mounted on the KV chassis in medium regiments of sixteen guns apiece and used to support the infantry divisions, while the remainder were used in Guards brigades with 65 guns apiece. The Soviets also deployed the BM-8 and BM-13 'Katyusha' multiple-rocket launchers (known to the Germans as the 'Stalin Organ') that mounted a number of rockets (up to 48), the most common being 82mm with a range of 6,000m and 132mm with a range of 9,250m, on a wheeled truck.

The Red Army still employed large numbers of cavalry units and had one cavalry brigade and 12 cavalry divisions in the order of battle for Operation *Berlin*. They were intended to give the Red Army some mobility over poor terrain, such as forests and marshes, which was not suitable for armoured vehicles. A cavalry corps usually consisted of two or three cavalry divisions and was given a great deal of additional firepower, in the form of between two and four tank regiments (70–140 tanks), an assault gun regiment and various artillery units. They were often paired with mechanized or tank corps to form special cavalry-mechanized groups.

SOVIET ORDER OF BATTLE

2ND BYELORUSSIAN FRONT – Marshal K. K. Rokossovsky

2nd Shock Army – ColGen I. I. Fedyurinsky
108th & 116th Rifle Corps

65th Army – ColGen P. I. Batov
18th, 46th & 105th Rifle Corps

70th Army – ColGen V. S. Popov
47th, 96th & 114th Rifle Corps

49th Army – ColGen I. T. Grishin
70th & 121st Rifle Corps
191st, 200th & 330th Rifle Divisions

19th Army
40th Guards, 132nd & 134th Rifle Corps

5th Guards Tank Army
29th Tank Corps

4th Air Army – ColGen K. A. Vershinin
4th Air Assault, 5th Air Bomber and 8th Air Fighter Corps

1ST BYELORUSSIAN FRONT – Marshal G. K. Zhukov

61st Army – ColGen P. A. Belov
9th Guards, 80th & 89th Rifle Corps

1st Polish Army – LtGen S. G. Poplowski
1st, 2nd, 3rd, 4th & 6th Polish Infantry Divisions

47th Army – LtGen F. I. Perkhorovitch
77th, 125th & 129th Rifle Corps

3rd Shock Army – ColGen V. I. Kutznetsov
7th Rifle Corps – MajGen V. A. Christov / ColGen Y. T. Chyervichenko
146th, 265th & 364th Rifle Divisions
12th Guards Rifle Corps – LtGen A. F. Kazanin / MajGen A. A. Filatov
23rd Guards, 52nd Guards & 33rd Rifle Divisions
79th Rifle Corps – MajGen S. I. Perevertkin
150th Rifle Division – MajGen V. M. Shatilov
171st Rifle Division – Col A. P. Negoda
207th Rifle Division – Col V. M. Asafov
9th Tank Corps – LtGen I. F. Kirichenko

5th Shock Army – Gen / ColGen N. E. Berzarin
9th Rifle Corps – MajGen / LtGen I. P. Rossly
230th, 248th & 301st Rifle Divisions
26th Guards Corps – MajGen P. A. Firsov
89th Guards, 94th Guards & 266th Rifle Divisions
32nd Rifle Corps – LtGen D. S. Zherebin
60th Guards, 295th & 416th Rifle Divisions

8th Guards Army – ColGen V. I. Chuikov
4th Guards Rifle Corps – LtGen V. A. Glazonov
35th Guards, 47th Guards & 57th Guards Rifle Divisions
28th Guards Rifle Corps – LtGen V. M. Shugeyev
39th Guards, 79th Guards & 88th Guards Rifle Divisions
29th Guards Rifle Corps – MajGen P. I. Zalizyuk
27th Guards, 74th Guards & 82nd Guards Rifle Divisions

69th Army – ColGen V. Y. Kolpakchi
25th, 61st & 91st Rifle Corps
117th & 283rd Rifle Divisions

33rd Army – ColGen V. D. Svotaev
16th, 38th & 62nd Rifle Corps
2nd Guards Cavalry Corps
95th Rifle Division

16th Air Army – ColGen S. I. Rudenko
6th & 9th Air Assault Corps
3rd & 6th Air Bomber Corps
1st Guards, 3rd, 6th & 13th Air Fighter Corps
1st Guards, 240th, 282nd & 286th Air Fighter Divisions
2nd & 11th Guards Air Assault Divisions
113th, 183rd, 188th & 221st Air Bomber Divisions
9th Guards & 242nd Air Night Bomber Divisions

18th Air Army – AVM A. Y. Golovanov
1st Guards, 2nd, 3rd & 4th Air Bomber Corps
45th Air Bomber Division
56th Air Fighter Division

1st Guards Tank Army – ColGen M. Y. Katukov
8th Guards Mechanized Corps – MajGen I. F. Drygemov
11th Guards Tank Corps – Col A. H. Babadshanian
11th Tank Corps – MajGen I. I. Jushuk

2nd Guards Tank Army – ColGen S. I. Bogdanov
1st Mechanized Corps – LtGen S. I. Krivosheina
9th Guards Tank Corps – MajGen A. F. Popov
12th Guards Tank Corps – MajGen M. K. Teltakov / Col A. T. Shevchenko

3rd Army – ColGen A. V. Gorbatov
35th, 40th & 41st Rifle Corps

1ST UKRAINIAN FRONT – Marshal I. S. Koniev

3rd Guards Army – ColGen V. N. Gordov
21st, 76th & 120th Rifle Corps
25th Tank Corps
389th Rifle Division

13th Army – ColGen N. P. Phukov
24th, 27th & 102nd Rifle Corps

5th Guards Army – ColGen A. S. Zhadov
32nd, 33rd & 34th Guards Rifle Corps
4th Guards Tank Corps

2nd Polish Army – LtGen K. K. Swiersczewski
5th, 7th, 8th, 9th & 10th Polish Infantry Divisions
1st Polish Tank Corps

52nd Army – ColGen K. A. Koroteyev
48th, 73rd & 78th Rifle Corps
7th Guards Mechanized Corps
213th Rifle Division

2nd Air Army – ColGen S. A. Krasovsky
1st Guards, 2nd Guards & 3rd Air Assault Corps
4th & 6th Guards Air Bomber Corps
2nd, 5th & 6th Air Fighter Corps
208th Air Night Bomber Division

3rd Guards Tank Army – ColGen P. S. Rybalko
6th Guards Tank Corps – MajGen V. A. Mitrofanov
7th Guards Tank Corps – MajGen V. V. Novikov
9th Mechanized Corps – LtGen I. P. Suchov

4th Guards Tank Army – ColGen D. D. Lelyushenko
5th & 6th Guards Mechanized Corps
10th Guards Tank Corps

28th Army – LtGen A. A. Luchinsky
20th, 38th Guards & 128th Rifle Corps

31st Army – LtGen V. K. Baranov
1st Guards Cavalry Corps

GERMAN FORCES

In contrast to the tight system of centralized control that characterized the Soviet chain of command, the Wehrmacht's chain of command was chaotic and messy. Adolf Hitler had vested in himself absolute control over the operations of the Wehrmacht, but had moved between desolately located command bunkers, gradually becoming divorced from reality. His immediate subordinates fought behind-the-scenes battles for power and influence and did nothing to try and inject a sense of reality about what was happening. Hitler had finally installed himself in the Führerbunker under the Reichs Chancellery on 16 January 1945. This facility suffered from a chronic lack of communications equipment and had not been set up to the same standard as the other headquarters that had been used around Europe during the war. It came with a one-man switchboard, a single radio transmitter and a radio telephone, which was dependent on having its aerial raised by means of a balloon.

His state of mind was not helped by stress, overwork, the attempted assassination or his failing health. Hitler had taken over command of both the armed forces and the army in December 1941. He had complicated the command structure even more by directing operations on the Eastern Front exclusively through the OKH (Oberkommando des Heeres – Army GHQ) while its responsibilities for other theatres had been passed to OKW (Oberkommando der Wehrmacht – Armed Forces GHQ), forcing the two to compete for scarce resources for their respective areas of responsibility. Additionally, Hitler's attitude to the General Staff was a major source of friction, as his system of unquestioning obedience to orders clashed with their system of mutual trust and exchanges of ideas, against a background of Hitler's class consciousness and the distrust of the General Staff following the assassination attempt.

Hitler's system of command was reflected in the state and composition of the German Armed Forces. One confusing practice was the use of corps and army headquarters that had been taken out of the line and placed in reserve, to control formations that had been rebuilt or newly raised, regardless of what branch of service they came from or their primary function. For example, the V SS Mountain Corps disposed only one Waffen SS division and no mountain troops, while the XI SS Panzer Corps consisted mainly of ordinary infantry units.

The quality of German infantry formations had steadily declined as the war had progressed, due to the number of casualties that had been suffered. From 1943 onwards, an increasing proportion of the infantry were being recruited from the fringes of Germany itself, from people known as Volksdeutsche, or ethnic Germans. Many senior commanders were worried as to the fighting qualities of these troops, as even units raised within Germany itself contained increasing numbers of Alsatians, Poles and other ethnic minorities who might not be overly enthusiastic about dying for the Third Reich. The German Panzer formations did not really suffer these problems to the same extent but were facing challenges with mobility as there was an ever growing shortage of fuel, made worse by the loss of access to the Rumanian and Hungarian oilfields. This also led to the curtailing of training that would have an increasingly detrimental effect on the quality of the Panzer troops. While German troops were still, on the whole, better than their Soviet equivalents, the large qualitative advantage the Germans had enjoyed in the opening phases of the Russo-German conflict had been significantly eroded.

German tank production had increased significantly during 1943 and 1944 but it still lagged behind Soviet industrial output. Its war industry had remained one of Germany's major weaknesses, despite Albert Speer's 1943 reforms. Even though Germany had out-performed the Soviet Union in heavy industrial output before the war, the victories of 1939 and 1940 had brought a great deal of Europe's industrial capacity under German control and the 1941 invasion had deprived the Soviet Union of much of its industrial potential. Even so, Germany had failed to keep pace with the Soviet Union, partly due to the effects of the Allied bombing offensive, but also because most of the leadership had failed to understand the importance of the economy in fighting a modern industrialized war. Germany had not mobilized her industries for full war production until very late on. The huge attrition of manpower in the First World War had given way to the huge attrition of material in this conflict, a challenge the Germans could not meet. This strategic blunder had become painfully obvious as the war had approached its closing stages.

The units available to the Germans included what was known as the Volkssturm, a form of Home Guard, that was intended for local defence and the construction of fortifications. It consisted of males aged sixteen and upwards who were capable of bearing arms in an emergency but not otherwise fit enough for active service. The majority, however, came from the upper age bracket and included many First World War veterans. They were organized into companies and battalions in their home districts but, with no standard establishment, battalions could range from 600 up to 1,500 in strength. Unit commanders were appointed by the party, some being veterans with military service and others purely local administrators.

The German ground forces were still primarily composed of army formations, although the abortive coup in July 1944 had led to a great purge of army officers, with political officers (NS – Führungsoffiziere) being appointed to formation headquarters to ensure the appropriate Nazi spirit. Reichsfuhrer-SS and Chef-der-Deutschen-Polizei (State SS and Police Chief) Heinrich Himmler had taken over control of the Reserve or Home Army, a position of considerable influence, and all new recruits had been assigned to the newly formed Volkswehr (People's Army) of Volksgrenadier and Volks Artillery units. They were considered to have greater political reliability and therefore had priority in men and equipment. After the army, the main organization that fielded ground units was the Waffen SS, also under Himmler. These, too, received priority of equipment over the army and had their own sources of supply, chiefly the slave labour camps. Unable to compete with the Wehrmacht with regard to the conscription laws, they turned to other sources of manpower and as a result, resembled the French Foreign Legion in composition. By 1945, the faith of even the Waffen SS Generals in Hitler was wavering and they no longer believed in final victory. Finally, there was the Berlin Garrison, which had its headquarters located opposite the Zeughaus (Arsenal) on the Unter-den-Linden. This command administered a motley collection of units, including military police, regular garrison troops, thousands of prisoners-of-war and slave-labourers, penal units, an engineer

Soviet SU122 tank destroyers in a Berlin suburb. The SU tank destroyers were essentially turretless versions of tanks such as the T-34 and JS-2, in the same way the Germans produced tank-destroyer versions of their own tanks, such as the Jagdpanzer IV and Jagdpanther. (From the fonds of the RGAKFD at Krasnogorsk)

battalion and the 'Grossdeutschland' Guard Regiment. The garrison formed part of Wehrkreis (Military District) III that had been administered by the headquarters of III Corps during peacetime. When III Corps went off to war, a deputy headquarters remained, which came under the Reserve or Home Army.

The Luftwaffe contributed not only GenObst Ritter von Greim's Luftflotte VI, but three types of ground formation. The first were the Fallschirmjäger, Germany's elite paratroopers. Many of the earlier replacements were from the non-flying branches of the service but were trained and indoctrinated into the elitist traditions of the service as these units were often used as shock troops alongside army formations. Later replacements however, including aircraftless crew did not have the benefit of such training. The second type of formation was the anti-aircraft artillery branch of the service that provided around 90 per cent of all German anti-aircraft defence personnel and was attached to all army formations down to divisional level. This branch of the Luftwaffe had started as an elite formation and remained so throughout the war, with batteries often acting as mobile artillery and fighting courageously until they were overrun. Up until the beginning of 1945, the main defence of Berlin had centred on its anti-aircraft capabilities in relation to the Allied bombing campaign. This defence was manned by the 1st 'Berlin' Flak Division and concentrated around three enormous flak towers that had been built in the parks at Friedrichshain, Humboldthain and the Zoo, each being a fortress with walls some six foot thick and steel doors over every aperture. There were also another dozen or so permanent anti-aircraft positions around the city, usually on the flat roofs of large well-built buildings. All of these could be expected to provide valuable support during the land battle, and could

GERMAN ORDER OF BATTLE

Those units directly involved with the defence of Berlin are shown in more detail.

OKW RESERVE (later allocated to the LVI Panzer Corps, 9th Army)

18th Panzergrenadier Division – MajGen Josef Rauch

ARMY GROUP 'VISTULA' – ColGen Gotthard Heinrici
III SS 'Germanic' Panzer Corps – SS LtGen Felix Steiner
    (divisions later allocated to the 9th Army)
    11th SS 'Nordland' Panzergrenadier Division – SS MajGen Jurgen Ziegler / SS MajGen Dr Gustav Krukenburg
    23rd SS 'Nederland' Panzergrenadier Division – SS MajGen Wagner

    (divisions later allocated to the 3rd Panzer Army)
    27th SS 'Langemarck' Grenadier Division
    28th SS 'Wallonien' Grenadier Division

3rd Panzer Army – Gen Hasso von Manteuffel
'Swinemunde' Corps – LtGen Ansat
    402nd & 2nd Naval Divisions
XXXII Corps – LtGen Schack
    'Voigt' & 281st Infantry Divisions
    549th Volksgrenadier Division
    Stettin Garrison
'Oder' Corps – SS LtGen von dem Bach / Gen Hörnlein
    610th & 'Klossek' Infantry Divisions
XXXXVI Panzer Corps – Gen Martin Gareis
    547th Volksgrenadier Division
    1st Naval Division

9th Army – Gen Theodor Busse
156th Infantry Division
541st Volksgrenadier Division
404th Volks Artillery Corps
406th Volks Artillery Corps
408th Volks Artillery Corps

CI Corps – Gen Wilhelm Berlin / LtGen Friedrich Sixt
    5th Light Infantry Division
    606th Infantry Division
    309th 'Berlin' Infantry Division
    25th Panzergrenadier Division
    '1001 Nights' Combat Group
LVI Panzer Corps – Gen Helmuth Weidling
    9th Fallschirmjäger Division – Gen Bruno Braüer / Col Harry Herrmann
    20th Panzergrenadier Division – Col / MajGen Georg Scholze
    'Müncheberg' Panzer Division – MajGen Werner Mummert
    1st & 2nd 'Müncheberg' Panzergrenadier Regts
XI SS Panzer Corps – SS Gen Mathias Kleinheisterkamp
    303rd 'Döberitz' Infantry Division
    169th Infantry Division
    712th Infantry Division
    'Kurmark' Panzergrenadier Division
Frankfurt an der Oder Garrison – Col / MajGen Ernst Biehler
V SS Mountain Corps – SS Gen Friedrich Jackeln
    286th Infantry Division
    32nd SS '30. January' Volksgrenadier Division
    391st Sy Division

ARMY GROUP CENTRE – GFM Ferdinand Schörner

4th Panzer Army – Gen Fritz-Herbert Gräser
    (later transferred to the 9th Army)
V Corps – LtGen Wagner
    35th SS Police Grenadier Division
    36th SS Grenadier Division
    275th Infantry Division
    342nd Infantry Division
    21st Panzer Division

12th Army – Gen Walther Wenck
XX Corps – Gen Carl-Erik Kohler
    'Theodor Körner' RAD Division
    'Ulrich von Hutten' Infantry Division
    'Ferdinand von Schill' Infantry Division
    'Scharnhorst' Infantry Division
XXXIX Panzer Corps – LtGen Karl Arndt
    (12 – 21 April 1945 under OKW with the following structure)
    'Clausewitz' Panzer Division
    'Schlageter' RAD Division
    84th Infantry Division
    (21 – 26 April 1945 under 12th Army with the following structure)
    'Clausewitz' Panzer Division
    84th Infantry Division
    'Hamburg' Reserve Infantry Division
    'Meyer' Infantry Division
XXXI Panzer Corps – LtGen Holste
    'von Hake' Infantry Division
    199th Infantry Division
    'V-Weapons' Infantry Division
XXXXVIII Panzer Corps – Gen Maximillian Reichsherr von Edelscheim
    14th Flak Division
    'Leipzig' Battle Group
    'Halle' Battle Group

Ungrouped Formations
'Friedrich Ludwig Jahn' RAD Division – Col Gerhard Klein / Col Franz Weller
'Potsdam' Infantry Division – Col Erich Lorenz

serve either as command posts or defensive positions, too. Third, there were the Luftwaffe Field Divisions that had been initially raised in 1942 from personnel skimmed from training organizations, flak and other ground service organizations, and committed as infantry.

The Germans had a variety of tanks, self-propelled guns and tank hunters (Jagdpanzers) available but the desperate situation they found themselves in meant that units were raised and equipped with anything that was available. The PzKw IV had seen series production throughout the war in various models and was now equipped with a 75mm L48 gun to enable it to stand up to the T-34/85. Most of the later German tanks had been inspired by the T-34, none more so than the 45-ton PzKw V 'Panther' which had well sloped amour, wide tracks and a 75mm L70 gun. This was followed by the 55-ton PzKw VI 'Tiger I', armed with an 88mm L56, and a 'Tiger II' with an 88mm L71 gun that was designed to dominate the battlefield. There were also tank hunters such as the Jagdpanzer IV with a 75mm L70 gun, the 'Jagdpanther' with an 88mm L71 gun and the Jagdpanzer VI 'Jagdtiger' with a 128mm L55 gun and a 70-ton weight. Some lighter models included the 'Hetzer' and 'Marder' vehicles, the former with a 75mm L48 gun and the latter with a 75mm L46 gun. Finally, there were the Sturmgeschütz III self-propelled guns and Flakpanzer armoured flak vehicles. The German armoured force was severely handicapped by the lack of fuel, the producion of which was a major target of the Allied bombing campaign.

However, one of the main continuing strengths of the Wehrmacht lay in its tactical skills, the flexibility of its command system and its ability to reorganize quickly, particularly in the defence. German field headquarters were kept small and well forward to maintain close contact with their subordinate commands. Officers were highly trained and able to make quick decisions, for their philosophy was that the unexpected could always be expected to happen and they would need to take decisive action rapidly and so there was a high degree of personal contact and mutual confidence in the command system.

OPPOSING PLANS

ALLIED PLANS

For Soviet Premier Josef Stalin, Berlin was the major prize of the Second World War and he feared that the Red Army might be beaten to the city by FM Bernard Montgomery's 21st Army Group. The British were advancing rapidly from Holland into North Germany, German resistance in the west having more or less collapsed after both the failure of the Ardennes offensive in December 1944 and the surrounding of Army Group B in the Ruhr Pocket in March 1945. This was averted, however, by Gen Dwight D. Eisenhower's (Supreme Allied Commander) change of mind. In September 1944 he had outlined his belief in a letter to his two principal subordinate commanders, Montgomery and Gen Omar Bradley, that he considered Berlin to be the main prize and that it was his desire to move on Berlin by the most direct and expeditious route. Montgomery wrote back and urged the Supreme Commander to decide what was necessary to go for Berlin, plan and organize the operation and then undertake it to finish the war as quickly as possible.

Eisenhower's strategy had always favoured a broad-front advance but there was a lack of decision about what would happen once the Allied forces had rejoined and created a unified front again, roughly in the area of Kassel, apart from a vague notion of continuing to advance eastwards. The British had always viewed Berlin as the central objective and had envisaged that their forces, 21st Army Group, would be the ones to make the main thrust to the north and east. Eisenhower effectively demolished this by continuing to plan for a broad-front offensive with the US 9th Army reverting to Bradley's command in order to help conduct mopping-up

Soviet artillery operating in close proximity to German positions, somewhere in the centre of Berlin, April 1945. The dust and clouds of debris in the background and the elevation of the gun suggest they are firing at the upper storeys of a nearby building, trying to winkle out German troops from their strongpoint. (IWM, FLM3350)

A Soviet soldier with a Panzerfaust. This weapon was a disposable, handheld anti-tank weapon that was issued in huge numbers to the German infantry and posed a very real threat to Soviet tanks, should they come into range. (From the fonds of the RGAKFD at Krasnogorsk)

operations in the Ruhr and then advance eastwards to an Erfurt–Leipzig–Dresden line, with Montgomery's 21st Army Group protecting the northern flank and Gen Jacob Devers' 6th Army Group protecting the southern flank. Eisenhower thus intended to concentrate the Western Allies' advance in the centre with Bradley in order to meet the Soviet advance around Dresden and cut Germany in two – as far as he was concerned, Berlin had become nothing but a geographical location. At the time Eisenhower made his decision, Montgomery's 21st Army Group was still 300 miles from Berlin and the Soviets, who had reached the River Oder, were less than 50 miles from the city; Model's Army Group B in the Ruhr still had to be properly dealt with; and Hitler might retire to the 'National Redoubt' in the Bavarian and Austrian mountains that might require many months and the expenditure of large resources to reduce. Given Eisenhower's insistence that military operations should be in pursuit of political aims, given Berlin's enormous importance as a political objective and given the fact that Berlin contained Hitler, whose capture or demise would destroy the German will to resist, it is difficult to understand why Eisenhower suddenly made a complete turnabout and pronounced Berlin as having no significance.

The pleasure with which this change of mind was received (in a communication sent to Stalin, the Combined Chiefs of Staff and the British Chiefs of Staff on 28 March) in Moscow was equal to the consternation in London. The British Chiefs of Staff were upset as they thought that by communicating directly with Stalin, he had usurped the authority of President Franklin D. Roosevelt, Prime Minister Winston S. Churchill, their Governments and their Chiefs of Staff. While Churchill had some sympathy for this view, he knew very well that Eisenhower's prestige in Washington at that moment was very high and that it was vital to try to elicit from the Soviets their views as to the best points of contact between the two armies. Churchill criticized the change of plan because it shifted the axis of advance – the continuation of the drive on Berlin was of paramount importance as the rapid advances by the Western Allies had surprised and annoyed the Soviets. Churchill had already seen not only the ending of the current great conflict but the beginnings of the next, with the Soviets already going back on promises that had been agreed at Yalta. The Allied Armies had to meet the Soviets as far east as they could get, and if possible take Berlin, as it was very likely that the Soviets would take Vienna. Eisenhower however, remained steadfast, supported by both Bradley and the US Combined Chiefs of Staff.

Stalin's reply to Eisenhower was broadly in line with the Supreme Allied Commander's plan in that:

- First, the Red Army and Western Allies should meet on the line of Erfurt–Leipzig–Dresden.
- Second, Berlin had lost its strategic importance and only secondary forces would be allotted to its capture.
- Third, the main thrust by Soviet forces would begin in the second half of May.
- Fourth, the Germans were reinforcing the Eastern Front with the 6th SS Panzer Army, as well as three divisions from Italy and two from Norway.

It is obvious that the second and third points were in fact deliberate falsifications by Stalin to try to hide what he was really planning – to enhance Soviet prestige and establish the Communist domination of Eastern and Central Europe by the Soviet Union by entering Berlin first. This was in fact borne out by what happened in reality. There is also the strong likelihood that Stalin's insistence that Berlin be taken quickly, before the Allies, was influenced not only by political issues but by strategic ones as well. Stalin was eager to get his hands on the Kaiser Wilhelm Institute in the southwest suburbs of Berlin before the Western Allies, as through his spy network he knew that the Americans were well advanced with their Manhattan Project, the programme to build an atomic bomb. His own nuclear programme, Operation *Borodino*, was lagging behind and Soviet scientists were keen to access whatever research the Germans had done. In the event, NKVD troops found almost three tons of Uranium Oxide, a material the Soviets had been short of and enough to give a substantial boost to their programme to build an atomic device. This desire to occupy Berlin first, despite already agreeing to share in its occupation after the city's surrender, would have dire consequences for the ordinary Soviet soldier.

Stalin, while at the Soviet Main Planning Conference on 1 April with Marshals Zhukov and Koniev, General Antonev (Soviet General Staff) and Gen Shtemenko (Main Operations Directorate), asked Shtemenko to read out a telegram. It indicated that the Western Allies were planning an operation to seize Berlin and that, with Montgomery's 21st Army Group already approaching the Elbe, they could get to the city before the Red Army (whether this was faulty intelligence or just a ploy of Stalin's is open to question). Both front commanders readily declared that they should be the one to take Berlin. Zhukov lay in the better position, immediately east of Berlin, with Koniev to his south, who would only be able to directly assault the German capital after a considerable amount of redeployment. Stalin, always willing to encourage the rivalry

Soviet self-propelled artillery and infantry crossing a bridge on their way to Berlin. Self-propelled artillery gave the Soviets a weapon system that could keep up with the tank armies once they had broken through the main German defences. (From the fonds of the RGAKFD at Krasnogorsk)

between the two men, knew that the operational boundary between the two fronts, as drawn by Stavka, ran from just south of Guben on the River Neisse via Michendorf to Schönebeck on the River Elbe. Stalin silently erased it after Lübben on the River Spree, implying that, after this point, whatever happened was up to the commanders - whoever reached there first, would have the first crack at the capital. To the north of Zhukov, the 2nd Byelorussian Front under Marshal Rokossovsky was still engaged in East Prussia but would continue its advance westward to the north of Berlin as soon as it was practicable. To the south of Koniev, the 4th (under ColGen I. E. Petrov, then Gen I. A. Yeremenko) and 2nd (under Marshal Rodion Y. Malinovsky) Ukrainian Fronts would continue to advance into Czechoslovakia and to the south of them, the 3rd Ukrainian Front under Marshal Fedor I. Tolbukhin would continue to drive west through Hungary and into Austria.

Both men had just 48 hours to come up with a draft plan. After weeks of heavy fighting, they had hoped to be able to stop, rest, re-equip and reinforce their commands before the start of the next big offensive in May (something that Stalin had indicated to Eisenhower as well) but it was obvious that Stalin intended them to move much sooner. The two commanders, who would be vying for first place in Berlin, approached the task in different ways. Zhukov, whose 1st Byelorussian Front was only 50 miles directly east of Berlin, already had a small bridgehead across the River Oder at Küstrin and would use over 140 searchlights to blind the defenders and almost 10,000 artillery pieces in a short sharp barrage of 30 minutes. Concealment was a real problem for Zhukov as the initial assault elements of the front (which contained four field and two tank armies, with another two field armies supporting the flanks) was packed into the small bridgehead and spring had come late this year with many trees still leafless and the ground sodden. Koniev on the other hand prepared to attack under cover of darkness with a barrage that would last 145 minutes. Overall, the Soviets deployed one gun for every 13 feet of front. The objectives for the bombardment and initial assaults were targeted with as much precision as possible, but despite extensive aerial and ground reconnaissance, Zhukov failed to identify the main line of resistance on the Seelow Heights and had to battle for four days in order to break through.

GERMAN PLANS

In February 1945, Adolf Hitler had decided to make Berlin a Festung, but failed to outline which troops were to be used for the defence of the city. The Commander, Wehrkreis III also became Commander, Berlin Defence Area – a logical step now that much of the district had been overrun or was now in effect on the front line. This meant that the officer with the least enviable task was GenLt Helmuth Reymann, who replaced the sick GenLt Bruno Ritter von Hauenschild. Reymann faced the culmination of the organizational chaos that characterized Hitler's government and was the third officer to be in charge of the Berlin Defence Area. He found that he had to deal with a whole gallery of different organizations, including the Hitler Youth, SS, Reserve Army, Army Group Vistula and the local Nazi Party organization which commanded the Volkssturm. This situation was

A German Panzerschrek in action. The Panzerschrek was closer to the American bazooka than the Panzerfaust as it could be reloaded after each shot. Such weapons gave the German infantry a way of taking on the enormous numbers of tanks the Soviets deployed. (Nik Cornish Library)

aggravated by the fact that the Wehrkreis Headquarters had refused to take the defence planning seriously and waged a paper war with the Defence Area Headquarters, although it was eventually evacuated before the battle and took no part in it.

Finally, however, a plan of sorts, formulated by Maj Sprotte, was issued on 9 March 1945 for the defence of Berlin. This 35-page document outlined that with the main threat coming from Soviet armour, the defence would naturally be constricted by the terrain both within and surrounding Berlin. Much of the ground would be suitable for mechanized movement, with a good network of roads and large areas of open sandy ground often screened by woodland. While there was a large number of streams, rivers, canals, ditches and irrigated fields that could provide temporary anti-tank obstacles, the only major obstacles to tank movement were the Havel Lakes in the west, the Spree River, Müggelsee and the Dahme River to the southeast. There was, however, a belt of woods and lakes at an average distance of 25 miles out from the city centre that could be adapted into a defensive perimeter. The system devised would be in addition to the plans prepared by Army Groups Vistula and Centre to defend the Oder–Neisse river line and incorporated a number of ideas put forward by both Hitler and Göbbels, as follows:

- A forward defence line in the east that used the natural barriers between the Alte Oder and Dahme rivers. This would have natural strength but only a few nominal field fortifications were built along its length.
- An obstacle belt that consisted of roadblocks on the major road junctions north and south of the city. Each one would be covered by a defensive position but due to the nature of the terrain, many of these were prone to being bypassed or dealt with at leisure.
- An Outer Defence Ring that would roughly follow the line of the city boundary with alternate fallback positions. This was some 60 miles in length and therefore could not be manned effectively given the manpower constraints, but consisted of fire trenches with covered positions along its length and every road that

A German soldier in a defensive position with two Mauser Kar98k rifles nearby. The Germans were extremely adept at defensive warfare, especially when it used fortifications, trenches, bunkers and other enhanced positions where they could take advantage of terrain to channel attacking forces into pre-arranged killing zones. (Nik Cornish Library)

entered the city was strongly barricaded and covered by a defensive position.

- An Inner Defence Ring based on the S-Bahn (the underground railway network) circuit. This was some 30 miles in length and based on much more substantial obstacles that included railway cuttings, elevations on vast pylons or deep-sided embankments that provided ready-made ramparts and anti-tank ditches and had defensive positions and roadblocks all the way around.
- An innermost defensive position, named 'Zitadelle' (Citadel), centred on the island formed by the Spree River and Landwehr Canal, with outlying bastions (called 'Ost' and 'West') around Alexanderplatz and the Knie (Ernst-Reuter-Platz), that covered the more important governmental buildings such as the Reichstag and Reichs Chancellery.

The area between the Outer Defence Ring and the Zitadelle would be split up into eight defence sectors, labelled 'A' to 'H', where it was intended that the defending forces would conduct a defence in depth. Each sector would have an officer in charge with the authority of a divisional commander.

Reymann and his Chief of Staff Obst Hans Refior immediately set to work to organize the defences and assigned Obst Lobeck the task. He had only one engineer battalion at his disposal but, after a consultation with Göbbels, two of the city's Volkssturm battalions were assigned to the task, as were personnel from the Organization Todt (civil engineering service) and Reichsarbeitsdienst (Labour Service) who were the only ones with proper tools and equipment. The city's officials managed to muster around 70,000 people per day on this task and, despite the overall lack of resources, managed a credible effort, with the best defences in the centre. Reymann, however, lacked the military infrastructure to properly develop the plan in depth, as well as the number of troops of the correct calibre to put the plan into operation as intended. The Nazi hierarchy had a completely different philosophy: if the Soviets managed to get to Berlin, they would be forced into a stalemate by a battle of attrition, just as the 6th Army had faced at Stalingrad. If they prevailed, then the German people would have shown themselves to be unworthy of their leadership and deserved extinction.

THE CAMPAIGN

16–19 APRIL 1945

At 05.00 on 16 April 1945, Operation *Berlin* started with an enormous artillery barrage on the forward German lines defending the Seelow Heights. After about 20 minutes, 143 searchlights were turned on to light the way for the assault formations, while the barrage moved on deeper into the German positions. In many instances, these added to the confusion as they threw up strange reliefs or failed to pierce the gloom ahead. Gradually, the tanks and self-propelled guns began to flounder over the marshy terrain, losing touch with the infantry and upsetting the coordination of the attack. As Chuikov's forces closed in on the Haupt Canal, the only bridges left standing were covered by German fire and the attack came to a complete stop as the Soviets tried to bring bridging equipment up, causing a massive traffic jam. Zhukov's forces managed to clear the first line of German defences, but another line was on top of the Seelow Heights themselves, which were extremely difficult for armour to traverse. As the tanks fanned out, seeking ways up the slope, they ran into the fortified strongpoints of Friedersdorf and Dolgelin. Zhukov then decided to commit his two tank armies in force to try and smash his way over the heights. The 1st Guards Tank Army would support the 8th Guards Army, while the 2nd Guards Tank Army would support the 5th Shock Army. The commitment of these units made the traffic problems even worse and hampered redeployment of the artillery

Soviet infantry rush past the body of a dead German soldier who was armed with an MP40 sub-machine gun. That sort of weapon, along with the Soviet PPSh41, was ideal for the kind of urban fighting that erupted all over Berlin as the Soviets closed in. (IWM, FLM3348)

Soviet infantry moving forward cautiously in what looks like difficult terrain, quite possibly in the area of Seelow and Müncheberg on the west bank of the Oder. The depth and preparedness of the German defences there would cause grave problems to Zhukov. (Central Museum of the Armed Forces, Moscow)

which was needed to support the infantry in their assaults. The attack continued day and night with the 1st Byelorussian Front gradually inching their way forward but failing to achieve a breakthrough. At this point Zhukov was well aware of Stalin's displeasure, the dictator having rounded furiously on the Front commander for committing his tank armies so early against Stavka's instructions, and that he was toying with the idea of allowing Koniev to let loose his tank armies on Berlin from the south and speeding up Rokossovsky's attack in order to assault Berlin from the northwest.

Zhukov regrouped his artillery and armour and continued the assault the next day. The 11th Guards Tank Corps and 8th Guards Mechanized Corps reached the railway line and took both Friedersdorf and Dolgelin but were stopped by counterattacks from the 'Kurmark' Panzergrenadier Division. The 3rd Shock Army continued its drive for Kunersdorf while other Soviet forces advanced north of Seelow and finally assaulted the town itself, a linchpin in the German defences. However, the Soviets could still not break through as their forward progress was slowed by numerous defensive positions, strongpoints and counterattacks. The German defences were beginning to crack under this intolerable pressure, though, and the 8th Guards Army managed to take Seelow by the end of the day. The next day the assault was renewed once again and by now the sheer weight of men, material and firepower was proving to be too much for the German defences, despite the staggering losses they had so far inflicted. The 9th Army was holding but its left flank was beginning to collapse and its right was now threatened by Koniev's break-through to the south. The LVI Panzer Corps held on for another day but desperately needed reinforcements, although it had been promised the 11th SS 'Nordlund' Panzergrenadier and 18th Panzer Divisions, neither of which arrived in time. Zhukov was determined to continue to pile on the pressure. The 47th Army attacked in the direction of Wriezen, the 3rd Shock Army attacked towards Kunersdorf and 5th Shock Army advanced towards Reichenberg and Münchehof, but all ran into the third line of German defences and came to a halt, as had the 69th Army. The only force to make any real progress was Chuikov's 8th Guards Army

THE ENCIRCLEMENT OF BERLIN, 16–28 APRIL 1945

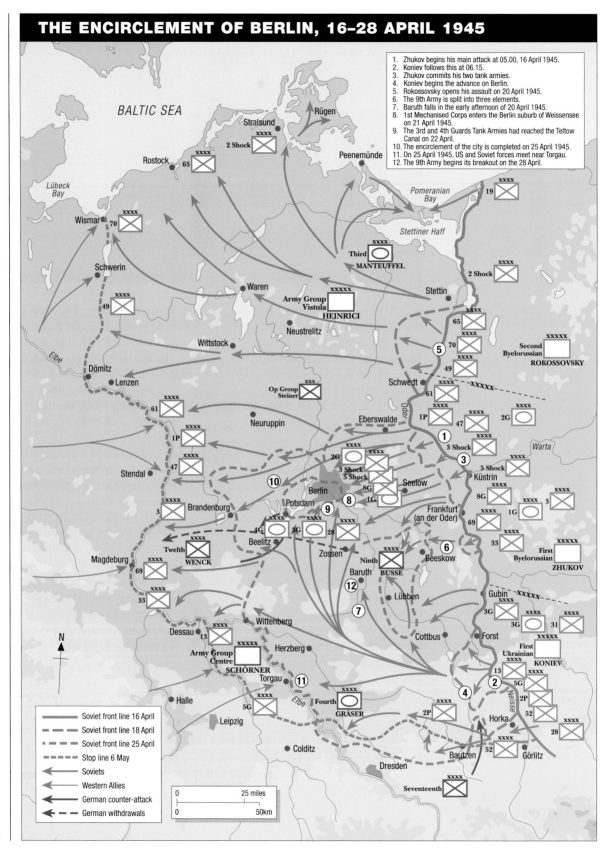

1. Zhukov begins his main attack at 05.00, 16 April 1945.
2. Koniev follows this at 06.15.
3. Zhukov commits his two tank armies.
4. Koniev begins the advance on Berlin.
5. Rokossovsky opens his assault on 20 April 1945.
6. The 9th Army is split into three elements.
7. Baruth falls in the early afternoon of 20 April 1945.
8. 1st Mechanised Corps enters the Berlin suburb of Weissensee on 21 April 1945.
9. The 3rd and 4th Guards Tank Armies had reached the Teltow Canal on 22 April.
10. The encirclement of the city is completed on 25 April 1945.
11. On 25 April 1945, US and Soviet forces meet near Torgau.
12. The 9th Army begins its breakout on the 28 April.

BALTIC SEA

Rügen

Stralsund

2 Shock

Peenemünde

Rostock

65

Lübeck Bay

Wismar

70

Pomeranian Bay

19

Stettiner Haff

Schwerin

Third
MANTEUFFEL

2 Shock

Waren

Stettin

49

Army Group
Vistula
HEINRICI

Neustrelitz

65

70

Second
Byelorussian
ROKOSSOVSKY

Wittstock

49

Elbe

Dömitz

Schwedt

61

Lenzen

Op Group
Steiner

Eberswalde

61

1P

47

2G

Neuruppin

1

3 Shock

Warta

1P

3

47

2G
3 Shock
5 Shock

Seelow

5 Shock
Küstrin

Stendal

Berlin

8G

8G

3

Potsdam

1G

69

3

Brandenburg

9

8

Frankfurt
(an der Oder)

1G

10

4G

3G

28

Beelitz

33

First
Byelorussian
ZHUKOV

Twelfth
WENCK

Zossen

Ninth
BUSSE

6

Beeskow

Magdeburg

69

Baruth

12

Lübben

Gubin

3G

33

7

Cottbus

Forst

3G

31

Dessau

13

Wittenberg

First
Ukrainian
KONIEV

Army Group
Centre
SCHÖRNER

Herzberg

13

5G

Halle

Torgau

11

Elbe

Fourth
GRÄSER

5G

2P

2

5G

2P

Leipzig

Horka

52

28

Colditz

52

Görlitz

Dresden

Bautzen

Seventeenth

N

Soviet front line 16 April
Soviet front line 18 April
Soviet front line 25 April
Stop line 6 May
Soviets
Western Allies
German counter-attack
German withdrawals

0   25 miles
0   50km

A photograph showing German troops in a line-up. The sodden nature of the ground is clearly visible. Spring was late to start in 1945 and the weather clearly contributed to the difficulties faced by the 1st Byelorussian Front as it attacked the Seelow Heights. (Nik Cornish Library)

that was heading towards Müncheberg. During the night, however, Kutznetsov's 3rd Shock Army managed to take the village of Batzlow with a surprise attack and this gap was exploited by Berzarin's 5th Shock Army. With the Soviet offensive now cutting deeply into the third line of defences, the 8th Guards Army attacked the town of Müncheberg on the 19th, taking the town by the late evening, which with the fall of Wriezen, meant that Zhukov had finally cracked all three German defence lines across a 45-mile front and could now make for Berlin.

Koniev's assault had started with his artillery opening up at 06.15 on 16 April, laying smoke for some 250 miles. After 40 minutes the assault battalions were sent in to cross the Neisse River at over 150 sites. Bridges were quickly laid and armour started to move across the river to support the infantry. As the day progressed, Koniev's forces managed to penetrate the German defences by up to nine miles across a 17-mile front. Koniev continued his attacks through the night and into the next day, drawing out the German tactical and operational reserves. His main assault went in at 09.00 after a short artillery bombardment and the 3rd and 4th Guards Tank Armies tore right through the German 4th Panzer Army and moved into open country. The 3rd and 5th Guards Armies on the flanks held off furious German counterattacks while the 13th Army followed the tanks. After a talk with Stalin, Koniev turned them on Berlin.

With Zhukov's breakthrough, the 9th Army was split into three sections. The CI Corps with their southern flank now exposed retired towards the Finow Canal, allowing the 61st and 1st Polish Armies to advance westwards. The LVI Panzer Corps was obliged to retire directly west towards Berlin and the only bridges that would enable it to rejoin the main body to the south, while Busse's immediate command was reduced to the Frankfurt-an-der-Oder Garrison, XI SS Panzer and V SS Mountain Corps, all of whom were trying to hold their original positions. The V Corps, consisting of the 21st Panzer, 35th SS Police Grenadier, 36th SS Grenadier, 275th Infantry and 342nd Infantry Divisions was assigned to him from the 4th Panzer Army.

The cost to the 1st Byelorussian Front of breaking through the German defences at Seelow were heavy, with the soldiers being exhausted after a four-day battle and the formation having reported over 33,000 **39** killed (the true cost being much greater) and the loss of a quarter of its armour. Zhukov determined that the 1st Guards Tank Army and 8th Guards Army would continue as a combined force along Reichstrasse 1 after which it would swing south over the Spree and Dahme Rivers, attacking the city from the south. The 2nd Guards Tank Army was split up, with the 9th Guards Tank Corps supporting the 47th Army, while the 1st Mechanized and 12th Guards Tank Corps would provide spearheads for the 3rd and 5th Shock Armies as they approached the northern suburbs. It would then reform, with the latter two corps taking over responsibility for a northern arc of the city alongside the two shock armies, who would cover the northeastern and eastern suburbs respectively. The 69th, 33rd and 3rd Armies would concentrate on the 9th Army and destroy it.

20 APRIL 1945

Hitler belatedly made Army Group Vistula responsible for the defence of the capital by placing the Berlin Defence Area in its area of responsibility. Heinrici immediately assigned this to the 9th Army but Busse argued that most of his formation was in no fit state to even get to Berlin, those that were left being in danger of encirclement, and so Heinrici rescinded the order. With the 9th Army split into three components, the only formation that was in a position to help was Weidling's LVI Panzer Corps, which was stretched to the limit. The 'Friedrich Ludwig Jahn' RAD Infantry Division was assigned to the garrison but it took all day just to find the divisional headquarters in a village north of Trebbin, and the division was later surprised by Soviet tanks and scattered. Heinrici then decided to move Steiner's III SS 'Germanic' Panzer Corps to cover his southern flank to counter the threat from the Soviet breakthrough. He would take over the remains of the CI Corps and the 25th Panzergrenadier Division, as well as being reinforced with the 3rd Naval Division and the 4th SS Police Grenadier Division that was supposedly forming in the area.

The Soviets were quickly advancing on the capital, with Koniev meeting very little resistance. The 3rd Guards Tank Army covered some 37 miles and took Baruth, almost reaching Zossen before the leading brigade of the 6th Guards Tank Corps ran out of fuel and was destroyed by Panzerfausts. This occurred close to the 'Maybach' bunker complex where OKW and OKH were waiting to evacuate. The 4th Guards Tank Army covered some 28 miles during daylight but encountered resistance around Jüterbog and Luckenwalde. The 1st Byelorussian Front continued to move forward with the 1st and 2nd Guards Tank Armies leading the way but being slowed by the continued effectiveness of the handheld anti-tank weapons liberally supplied to the German infantry as well as the presence of the LVI Panzer Corps. The 2nd Byelorussian Front started their assault across the west branch of the Oder that morning but poor weather favoured the defence and the only unit that gained a bridgehead was the 65th Army.

Heinrici spent most of the day trying to restore order to the disorganized body of troops retreating from the Soviet breakthrough. By the evening he had managed to form something of a defence line along the line of the autobahn after an appeal to OKH for troops to hold the Havel River between Oranienburg and Spandau, he was allocated the 'Müller' Brigade. Back in Berlin, the Führer celebrated his 56th birthday, with a gathering of his entourage including von Ribbentrop, Himmler, Göring, Dönitz, Speer, Göbbels, Axmann, Keitel, Jodl and Bormann. The US Army Air Force added its salute with a raid by 299 B-17 bombers while the RAF had made their last attack on the city the previous night.

21 APRIL 1945

The 21 April saw the 2nd Guards Tank Army crossing the autobahn ring to the northeast of the city and advancing towards the city on a broad front, with the 1st Mechanized Corps ending up in Weissensee and the 12th Guards Tank Corps near Hohenschönhausen, but were mixed up with troops from the 3rd and 5th Shock Armies to either side of them. Towards the end of the day, they swung in a wide flanking movement in a north-westerly direction to reach their allotted sectors for the envelopment of the city. The 8th Guards and 1st Guards Tank Armies were also advancing towards the city from the Rüdersdorf–Erkner area and now received orders to swing away to the southwest in order to approach the city from the south and southeast, and the 11th Tank Corps was transferred to support the 5th Shock Army in its forthcoming operations. These orders would take time to implement, however, as many troops were caught up in fighting, while the nature of terrain limited movement. The 3rd Guards Tank Army reached Königs Wusterhausen, thereby completing the encirclement of the 9th Army. Koniev directed the 28th Army to seal off the pocket instead of the 13th Army, while Zhukov moved the 69th Army from the Oder along with the 3rd Army to apply pressure on the 9th Army from the north.

Soviet bombers over Berlin. These aircraft are either Petlyakov Pe-2s or Tupolev Tu-2s, both of which were light attack aircraft that could carry 3,000kg of bombs. The Soviets rarely undertook strategic bombing, concentrating the efforts of the air force on tactical and operational objectives in support of the ground forces. (Topfoto/Topham)

SEELOW HEIGHTS (pages 42–43)

The speed of the Soviet offensive across the River Vistula in January 1945 had left them with a number of bridgeheads across the Oder River by the end of the campaign in early March 1945. The Germans, aware that they needed a secure river line to stand any chance of holding the Soviet juggernaut when it started to move again, launched a number of determined counterattacks to eliminate these bridgeheads, whereas the Soviets fully appreciated their value in the up-and-coming attack on the capital of the Third Reich. The German attacks ultimately proved futile and so they turned their attention to preparing a defence in depth to meet the coming storm. The Soviets gradually expanded their bridgeheads until they coalesced into one, cutting off Küstrin. With the conclusion of operations in East Pomerania, the bulk of 1st Byelorussian Front returned to the Oder, while 2nd Byelorussian Front was still involved in reducing German resistance in East Prussia. On 1 April 1945, Stalin gave orders to commence Operation *Berlin* on 16 April, with the objective of reaching the Elbe by the May Day holiday, giving the commanders only some two weeks to prepare for an offensive that would usually require two to three months. The Soviets faced a difficult task in reinforcing, restocking and resupplying their forces and could just about gather some two-and-a-half million men to face one million defenders. This was hardly the necessary ratio of forces normally required for such an operation but, by this time, both the Germans and Soviets were coming to the end of their manpower reserves. The main operation would be conducted by the 1st Byelorussian and

1st Ukrainian Fronts, supported by the 2nd Byelorussian Front to the north after it had finished its operations in East Prussia. These were faced by the 3rd Panzer Army and 9th Army from Army Group 'Weichsel' (Vistula) in the north and 4th Panzer Army from Army Group 'Mitte' (Centre) in the south, while a new 12th Army was forming to cover the exposed front along the Elbe. The attack started as planned in the early hours of 16 April (1) and, while Koniev's 1st Ukrainian Front managed to achieved the desired break-through fairly quickly, Zhukov's 1st Byelorussian Front (2) faced a much more difficult task in attempting to pierce the German defences along the Seelow Heights (3). The attack started with a staggering artillery barrage (4) after which searchlights were turned onto to blind the German defenders. These only caused confusion and the barrage was only partially effective as the Germans had withdrawn their troops from the 1st line of defences (5). The first waves of Soviet tanks and infantry (6) had difficulty moving over the river valley (7) as the area had been deliberately flooded by the Germans turning the marshy ground into a water-logged morass (8), while the waterways, raised roads and railway lines either tended to form obstacles to be crossed or channelled the movement of the attacking forces along them. In the area between Letschin and Seelow, the forward elements of the 5th Shock Army and 8th Guards Army came up against the prepared defences of the 9th Fallschirmjäger (9) and 20th Panzer Grenadier Divisions, which inflicted severe casualties, bringing the attack to a standstill and forcing Zhukov to commit his armoured reserves in order to try and force the pace. (Peter Dennis)

The LVI Panzer Corps had been forced to retire due to Soviet pressure and eventually moved back to the line of Köpenick–Marzahn. 'Seydlitz Troops' had been active in spreading rumours and giving out false orders for formations to re-assemble at other locations outside the city and some in the Führerbunker thought that this is where LVI Panzer Corps had indeed moved to. This caused both Busse and Hitler to order Weidling's arrest and execution, although for different reasons. Weidling, meanwhile, was having his own problems with SS Brigadeführer Joachim Ziegler who was unhappy about serving under a Wehrmacht commander and wanted to pull his 11th SS 'Nordlund' Panzergrenadier Division back into the city. Soviet siege and heavy artillery started to shell the city centre, causing considerable alarm, and the flak towers engaged Soviet batteries in the suburb of Marzahn. FM Schörner arrived in Berlin to report on the progress of his counterattack, which was causing a great deal of trouble to Koniev's 1st Ukrainian Front, as did Gen Wenck who had come to report that the XXXIX Panzer Corps were trying to relieve the 11th Army trapped in the Harz Mountains. Hitler then ordered Steiner to conduct a counterattack to relieve Berlin and every possible resource be made available to him. The Germans managed to raise the equivalent of one-and-a-half infantry divisions from rear area troops and Luftwaffe ground personnel but of course they lacked the training and heavy weapons for such a task. Most of Steiner's command was already engaged along the Finow Canal and so he was forced to wait for the 3rd Naval Division coming from the coast.

22 APRIL 1945

The 22 April saw Krebs contacting Heinrici with permission for the Frankfurt-an-der-Oder Garrison to abandon the city and fall back to the 9th Army, where Busse had established an all-round defensive position, helped by the terrain in the area. Hitler ordered the 9th Army to cooperate with the 12th Army in making deep counterattacks into the enemy's flank, but Busse was already preparing his force for a breakout, as suggested by Heinrici. Steiner still had had no additional regular formations with which to conduct his relief effort and was still having to defend the town of Oranienburg and the Ruppiner Canal. Zhukov's northern screening force, led by the 9th Guards Tank Corps and 125th Rifle Corps, after a bad start, moved through Zepernick, Schönlinde, Mühlenbeck and Schönfliess to reach the bridge at Hennigsdorf. The 1st Polish Army had cleared the area between Biesenthal and Bernau and moved up to the canal in front of Oranienburg, attacking the town that night, while the 61st Army had cleared the area south of the line of canals. Meanwhile the 8th Guards Army and 1st Guards Tank Army entered the suburbs of Dahlwitz, Schöneiche, Fichtenau and Rahnsdorf, while Marshal Koniev's forces made rapid progress due to the open nature of the terrain and the uncoordinated and scattered resistance. The 4th Guards Tank Army moved the 5th Guards Mechanized Corps to form a protective screen along the line of Beelitz, Treuenbrietzen and Kropstädt, to be reinforced by the 13th Army. The 6th Guards Mechanized Corps reached Beelitz and the 10th Guards Tank Corps advanced through Saarmund and Schenkenhorst to seal off the approaches to Potsdam at Caputh and

ATTACK ON THE SEELOW HEIGHTS
SOVIET OPERATIONS 14 – 19 APRIL 1945

Soviet forces eventually broke through German defences on the Seelow Heights, but at a terrible cost to men and materiel.

Note: Gridlines are shown at intervals of 5 kilometers

GERMAN FORCES

9th Army (Busse):
CI Corps (Berlin / Sixt):
A 25th Panzer Grenadier Division
B 606th 'Berlin' Infantry Division
C 309th 'Berlin' Infantry Division (the Corps also had the 5th Lt Infantry Division under its command, deployed northwest of the 606th, facing the 61st Army)

LVI Panzer Corps (Weidling):
D 9th Fallschirmjäger
E 20th Panzer Grenadier Division
F 'Müncheberg' Panzer Division

XI SS Panzer Corps (Kleinheisterkamp):
G 'Kurmark' Panzer Grenadier Division
H 169th Division
I 303rd 'Döberitz' Division
J 712th Infantry Divisions

Army Troops:
K 156th Infantry Division
L 541st Volks Grenadier Division

SOVIET FORCES

1st Byelorussian Front (Zhukov)
47th Army (Perkhorovitch):
1 77th Rifle Corps
2 125th Rifle Corps
3 129th Rifle Corps

3rd Shock Army (Kutznetsov):
4 7th Rifle Corps
5 12th Guards Rifle Corps
6 79th Rifle Corps
7 9th Tank Corps

5th Shock Army (Berzarin):
8 9th Guards
9 26th Guards
10 32nd Rifle Corps

8th Guards Army (Chuikov):
11 4th Guards
12 28th Guards
13 29th Guards Rifle Corps

1st Guards Tank Army (Katukov)

2nd Guards Tank Army (Bogdanov)

3rd Army (Gorbatov)

69th Army (Kolpakchi)

▼ EVENTS

1. **Waterways would prove important in the development of any attack, generally either forming an obstacle to be crossed or channelling movement for the attacker. The Germans had deliberately flooded the area, turning the marshy lowland into a morass.**

2. **Marshal Georgi Zhukov's 1st Byelorussian Front had some 768,000 troops and 3,000 tanks, supported by over 14,000 guns.**

3. **The Soviets put a great deal of effort in preparing, logistically for the attack. The Küstrin bridgehead was packed with men, equipment and supplies, which were brought in by rail.**

4. **Facing this juggernaut was General Theodor Busse's 9th Army with 220,000 men and 512 tanks and self-propelled guns, later to be reinforced by three SS Panzer Grenadier Divisions.**

5. **On 14 and 15 April 1945, Zhukov uses reconnaissance groups of up to regimental strength along the whole of the line.**

6. **The Soviet artillery finally opened up in the early hours of 16 April and the searchlights (from Moscow's anti-aircraft defences) turned on shortly after. The effect was complete confusion. (03.00, 16 April 1945)**

7. **The Germans had in fact evacuated the first line of defence so the barrage was wasted on already empty positions.**

8. **The 3rd Shock, 5th Shock and 47th Armies had to contend with the main German line of defence either side of Letschin. (16 April)**

9. **The 69th Army sought to achieve a break-through north of Lebus, but the attack was contained by a counterattack by the 'Kurmark' Panzer Grenadier Division. (16 April)**

10. **Zhukov then released his armoured reserves but this only tended to make matters worse as the already clogged up roads were brought to a standstill. (11.00, 16 April)**

11. **The 4th Guards Rifle Corps finally managed to gain a foothold on the Heights behind Werbig and occupy the railway station south of Seelow. (Evening, 16 April)**

12. **28th Guard Corps launched its attack towards the village of Dolgelin but was stopped in its tracks by an antitank barricade and six Tiger tanks. (17 April)**

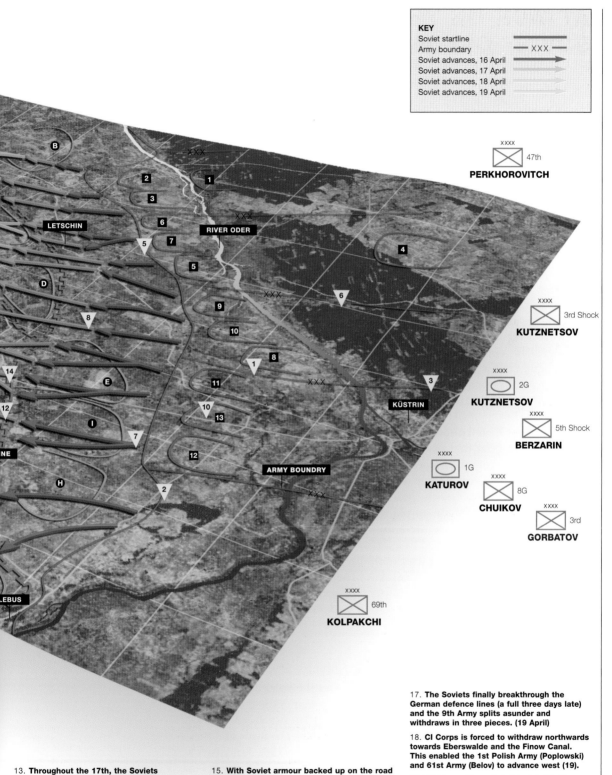

XXXX
47th
PERKHOROVITCH

LETSCHIN

RIVER ODER

XXXX
3rd Shock
KUTZNETSOV

XXXX
2G
KUTZNETSOV

KÜSTRIN

XXXX
5th Shock
BERZARIN

XXXX
1G
KATUROV

ARMY BOUNDRY

XXXX
8G
CHUIKOV

XXXX
3rd
GORBATOV

XXXX
69th
KOLPAKCHI

EBUS

NE

13. Throughout the 17th, the Soviets continued to exert pressure on the centre of the German defences and late in the day finally managed to breakthough the first line of defences either side of Seelow.

14. The Soviets finally take the town of Seelow, early on 18 April. (Morning, 18 April)

15. With Soviet armour backed up on the road into Müncheberg, a counterattack from the Müncheberg Panzer Division supported by the Luftwaffe inflicts terrible casualties. (18 April)

16. Zhukov is forced to amalgamate 8th Guards and 1st Guards Tank Army due to the horrendous losses suffered. (18 April)

17. The Soviets finally breakthrough the German defence lines (a full three days late) and the 9th Army splits asunder and withdraws in three pieces. (19 April)

18. CI Corps is forced to withdraw northwards towards Eberswalde and the Finow Canal. This enabled the 1st Polish Army (Poplowski) and 61st Army (Belov) to advance west (19).

20. LVI Panzer Corps is left isolated in the centre and has to retreat directly towards Berlin.

21. Busse's immediate command is reduced to the XI SS Panzer Corps, V SS Mountain Corps and the Frankfurt Garrison.

Soviet infantry cutting barbed wire in front of a German defensive position. Just as the 1st Byelorussian Front had had difficulty breaking through the German defences on the Seelow Heights, so it took the 2nd Byelorussian Front a week to break through 3rd Panzer Army's lines on the Oder. (Central Museum of the Armed Forces, Moscow)

Babelsburg. The 3rd Guards Tank Army, after forcing the Notte Canal near Zossen, continued to advance on Berlin on a broad front, with leading elements of two corps having reached the Teltow Canal by dusk.

At the daily conference in the Führerbunker, Hitler realized, despite the General Staff trying to drag the briefing out as long as possible, that Steiner had not even issued orders to begin the attack. He flew into a terrible rage, which barely abated so that he could declare his intention to remain in Berlin until the bitter end. He then went back to his private quarters where he telephoned Göbbels to invite him and his family into the bunker, an offer that was readily accepted. A large number of staff chose the opportunity to leave for Berchtesgaden, and a number of metal boxes were despatched with them containing Hitler's private papers. He then summoned Jodl and Keitel and told them of his intention to commit suicide should the Soviets take the city and that he had no more orders to give them and they should refer to the Reichs Marshal. However, he decided to examine possible means of saving the situation and to take direct responsibility for the defence of Berlin himself, relieving Army Group Vistula of the task, whereupon Göbbels decided to relieve GenLt Reymann of command of the Berlin Defence Area and assigned him to command the Potsdam Garrison.

23 APRIL 1945

On the 23rd, both sides were forced to reconsider their actions and assess what the campaign held in store for them. The Soviets looked to the fact they would be moving into an increasingly more urban landscape, with all the advantages that would confer on the defender, the Germans that they would now have to prepare for a siege. Wenck, whose 12th Army had a boundary that extended from the junction of the Havel and Elbe rivers in the north to just below Leipzig in the south, was briefed by Keitel as to the Führer's orders. The army consisted of the XXXIX Panzer Corps under GenLt Karl Arndt, but only from the 21 to 26 April after which it would transfer to the newly forming 21st Army, XXXXI Panzer Corps under

GenLt Rudolf Holste, XX Corps under GenLt Carl-Erik Köhler and XXXXVIII Panzer Corps under GenLt Maximilian Freiherr von Edelscheim, which was the army reserve. Wenck interpreted his orders as rescuing the 9th Army, as well as the thousands of refugees that were trapped with them as well as holding open an escape route for as many people as possible. It was fortunate that many of the supply barges traversing the country had become stuck here so Wenck was not short of ammunition, fuel or food. Keitel then reported this to Hitler at the Führerbunker who was impatient as to when the formations would start moving. This merely highlights the almost complete detachment from reality in which Hitler and his immediate staff operated and which Keitel did nothing to dispel.

Some reinforcements managed to get through to the city (as they would until the 24th), including the 'Grossadmiral Dönitz' Naval Battalion under Commander Franz Kuhlmann. There was concern that the Soviets might try to infiltrate by means of the U-Bahn and S-Bahn tunnels and so the traffic was stopped in order for barricades to be built, as well as demolitions being prepared at certain points to flood the tunnels, despite the presence of civilians and four hospital trains. The LVI Panzer Corps had moved across the Spree the previous night and into the suburb of Rudow. Weidling was preparing to move south again in order to support the 9th Army's northern flank but found that these orders from Gen Busse had been cancelled and the corps was to move into Berlin and Weidling was to take over defence of the city. Even so, there was little he could do except redistribute his forces around the city to beef up the local defence wherever possible, use the corps communications net to bolster those of the city's, augment the Berlin Defence Area Headquarters staff with officers from the corps' staff and reorganize the defence sector staffs. However, the Germans simply did not have the manpower available to implement Reymann's original plan as it was intended. The defence sector commands were now fully involved with the enemy, and were handicapped both by lack of resources and a lack of communications, both horizontally and vertically, which hampered coordination. Weidling, therefore, moved his command post to the Berlin Defence Area Headquarters on the

Hohenzollerndamm with an eye to moving it again more centrally, either to the flak control tower in the Tiergarten or Bendlerstrasse.

The 3rd Panzer Army was still holding Rokossovsky's forces on the Oder but was rapidly approaching breaking point. It was obvious to Heinrici that it would not be able to hold out much longer and so he started to plan for their withdrawal westwards in order to surrender to the Western Allies. Steiner continued to hold the line of canals on the southern flank but, when the Soviets outflanked Oranienburg, he had to man the Ruppiner Canal at the expense of the town. Heinrici then received orders from Keitel (on behalf of the Führer) for the XXXXI Panzer Corps to block the Soviet advance westward and that Steiner was to mount an immediate effort to relieve Berlin and cut off Zhukov's thrust across the Havel. He would be reinforced by the 7th Panzer and 25th Panzergrenadier Divisions, neither of which were available yet, the latter in fact coming from the end of his own line as he had been given permission to abandon the Eberswalde bridgehead. It was the 47th Army, with the 9th Guards Tank Corps (from 2nd Guards Tank Army) and 7th Guards Cavalry Corps that had indeed crossed the Havel, to act as a screening force and complete the encirclement of the city, reaching Nauen early in the day. The 125th Rifle Corps then moved up to Spandau and Gatow airfield, while the 77th Rifle Corps moved south, elements of which looked to link up with the 4th Guards Tank Army. The cavalry fanned out, scouring the countryside for resistance.

The encircling formations worked their way into the Berlin suburbs to the north and the east, learning the techniques of urban fighting as they went. The suburbs, however, would offer a different experience from the dense urban landscape of the city centre, but both sides made mistakes, although it was easier for the Soviets to recover from theirs with the resources they had to hand. The 1st Mechanized Corps (2nd Guards Tank Army) moved through Hermsdorf, Waidmannslust and Wittenau, while the 12th Guards Tank Corps advanced through Lübars, Blankenfelde and Rosenthal to take up position alongside the 79th Rifle

SQUEEZING THE BERLIN POCKET, 23–28 APRIL 1945

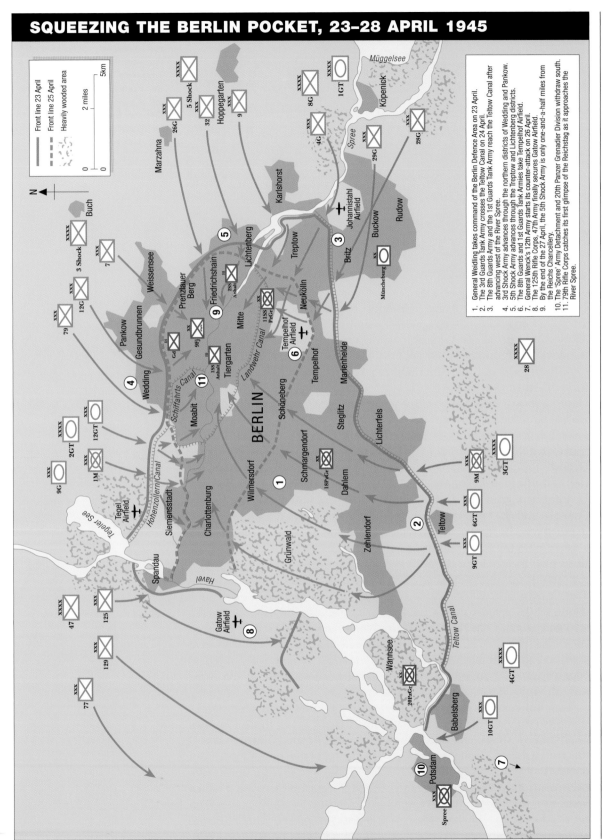

Legend
- Front line 23 April
- Front line 25 April
- Heavily wooded area

0 — 2 miles
0 — 5km

1. General Weidling takes command of the Berlin Defence Area on 23 April.
2. The 3rd Guards Tank Army crosses the Teltow Canal on 24 April.
3. The 8th Guards Army and the 1st Guards Tank Army reach the Teltow Canal after advancing west of the River Spree.
4. 3rd Shock Army advances through the northern districts of Wedding and Pankow.
5. 5th Shock Army advances through the Treptow and Lichtenberg districts.
6. The 8th Guards and 1st Guards Tank Armies take Tempelhof Airfield.
7. General Wenck's 12th Army starts its counter-attack on 26 April.
8. The 125th Rifle Corps, 47th Army finally secures Gatow Airfield.
9. By the end of the 27 April, the 5th Shock Army is only one-and-a-half miles from the Reichs Chancellery.
10. The 'Spree' Army Detachment and 20th Panzer Grenadier Division withdraw south.
11. 79th Rifle Corps catches its first glimpse of the Reichstag as it approaches the River Spree.

Corps from 3rd Shock Army, fighting in Niederschönhausen, while the 7th Rifle Corps was still engaged in Hohenschönhausen. The 5th Shock Army closed up to the fallback positions in defence sector 'A', taking Biesdorf and Kaulsdorf while its 9th Rifle Corps moved southwest and took Karlshorst and the Rummelsburg Power Station. The 4th Guards Rifle Corps (8th Guards Army) took the industrial area of Oberschönweide and prepared to cross the Spree at Johannisthal. The 29th Guards Rifle Corps captured a bridge over the Spree into Aldershof, as well as Köpenick with its bridges across the Spree and Dahme. The 3rd Guards Tank Army spent the day regrouping south of the Outer Defence Ring and waited for elements of the 28th Army to join them, the remainder being caught up in the 9th Army's encirclement and breakout.

Elsewhere, the 4th Guards Tank Army continued to close in on Potsdam and try to link up with the 47th Army, although no effort was made to cross the line of the Havel. The 13th and 5th Guards Armies were closing in on the Elbe, the former at Wittenberg, the latter near Torgau. Koniev decided to leave the 34th Guards Rifle Corps in the area to await the Americans and redirected the 32nd Guards Rifle and 4th Guards Tank Corps into reserve in order that they might participate in a counterstrike against the German forces attacking towards Spremberg who had split the 52nd and 2nd Polish Armies apart and created havoc in their rear areas. It is obvious at this point that Koniev's forces were stretched to the limit and he had only a small reserve with which to counter any movement by the 9th and 12th Armies – even his 6th Army was still engaged in besieging Breslau.

Gen Koller arrived at Berchtesgaden and briefed Göring on events in the Führerbunker the previous day. He advised Göring to take control as Hitler had apparently abandoned leadership of the government and the armed forces. Göring was reluctant as he had been out of favour but decided to send a telegram to Hitler informing him that he would take over control of the country and armed forces, as per the Law of Succession of 1941, if he had not heard from him by 22.00, after which he would assume he had lost his freedom of action. The telegram arrived in the Führerbunker and was shown to Hitler by Bormann who suggested that Göring was trying to seize power for himself. Hitler flew into a rage and ordered Göring and his staff put under house arrest. This episode was witnessed by Albert Speer who had flown into Berlin in order to confess to Hitler that he had been obstructing the Scorched Earth policy, something that might have cost him his head, but which provoked only a mild response from the Führer.

24 APRIL 1945

Weidling's redeployment of the LVI Panzer Corps bolstered the weak defence that he had found there, after taking up his new appointment. The 20th Panzergrenadier Division had been forced onto Wannsee 'Island' and so the 18th Panzergrenadier Division was moved out of reserve to replace it. The 9th Fallschirmjäger Division would support the northern sectors having based itself in the Humboldthain Flak Tower, the 'Müncheberg' Panzer Division would assist in the defence of Tempelhof Airport, while the 11th SS 'Nordland' Panzergrenadier Division moved to the Neukölln–Kreuzberg area.

Meanwhile, in the Führerbunker, Hitler had seemingly recovered from his breakdown of the 22nd and ordered that OKW was to be responsible to him for the conduct of all operations, ending the illogical OKW / OKH share of responsibilities. He sent word for GenObst Ritter von Greim (Commander, Luftflotte VI) to report to him. Von Greim, puzzled by this development and, unaware of Göring's disgrace, went to consult with Koller whom he knew to be at Berchtesgaden. Keitel revisited XXXXI Panzer Corps, where Holste sought to blame the slowness of his redeployment on the lack of suitable transport.

The 2nd Guards Tank Army continued its advance southwards, crossing the Jung- fernheide and reaching the Hohenzollern Canal during the afternoon. Under the cover of some woods, they quickly prepared a crossing and, by nightfall, several combat groups had established

Soviet troops manoeuvre an artillery piece into position. All formations up to front level were liberally supplied with artillery for the Berlin operation; this was useful given that many German defensive positions were in enormous, solidly built buildings that could absorb a tremendous amount of fire. (IWM, FLM3349)

themselves on the edge of Siemensstadt, a large industrial complex built by the Siemens Company. The 3rd Shock Army faced stiff resistance, however, upon reaching the canal, with the 79th Rifle Corps having moved through Reinickendorf and taking the deserted 'Hermann Goring' Barracks, while the 12th Guards Rifle Corps had advanced through Wedding and came up against German strongpoints at the Wedding S-Bahn station and the Humboldthain Flak Tower. Only the 7th Rifle Corps continued to make relatively unimpeded progress down the two roads that led to Alexanderplatz. The 5th Shock Army continued to advance westwards, with the 26th Guards and 32nd Rifle Corps on either side of the Frankfurter Allee, clearing the Schlachthof (Abattoir) Complex just inside the Inner Defence Ring. The 9th Rifle Corps crossed the Spree into Treptow Park from Rummelsburg and, after forcing back elements of the 11th SS 'Norlund' Panzergrenadier Division, started to move parallel to both the Spree and Landwehr Canal.

The 8th Guards Army (with 1st Guards Tank Army) was busy shifting westwards in order to attack Berlin from the south and ran into elements of the 3rd Guards Tank Army

Soviet infantry and tanks (probably T-34/85s) advance down a main street in Berlin, during the advance towards the city centre. While this street is relatively wide, allowing some degree of manoeuvre, many streets were much narrower and excellent sites for an anti-tank team to ambush a Soviet column. (Topfoto/Topham)

and therefore inadvertently linked up with 1st Ukrainian Front, before moving up to the Teltow Canal. This sent enormous shockwaves up through Army and Front command levels, with Zhukov hardly believing what he had heard and sending some officers to find out who they were and what they were doing. Apart from the damage to Zhukov's pride, this underlines the lack of communication between the higher levels of command and the continued distrust between Zhukov and Koniev. With his intentions now in the open, Stalin laid down the inter-front boundary as running from Lubben, through Teupitz, Mittenwalde and Mariendorf to the Anhalter Railway Station, from where it continued to the east of the Reichstag, giving Koniev the opportunity to reach it first from the south. Meanwhile, 3rd Guards Tank Army conducted its assault across the Teltow Canal, which had patchy success. The 9th Mechanized Corps initially established a bridgehead at Lankwitz that was wiped out by a German counterattack but the 6th Guards Tank Corps established one at Teltow, as did the 7th Guards Tank Corps to its left, although resistance was such Koniev chose not to expand it for the time being. This resistance was due to the assistance given to the local defence by the remnants of the 20th Panzergrenadier Division, followed by the 18th Panzergrenadier Division, which with over 6,000 men, two 'Tiger' tanks, 20 PzKw IV tanks and 25 APCs, was still a powerful force. The 4th Guards Tank Army continued northeast, with the 10th Guards Tank Corps reaching the outskirts of Potsdam and the 6th Guards Mechanized Corps reaching Brandenburg.

Soviet artillery opens up on a German strongpoint at close range. The Soviets made great use of artillery during the urban fighting and assigned engineers to clear ways through blocked streets and back gardens so the guns could keep up with the advancing troops. (IWM, FLM3346)

Elsewhere, the 13th Army reached Wittenberg on the Elbe and ran into the encamped XX Corps from Wenck's 12th Army. The fighting that was sparked off was so intense, Koniev thought that this was the anticipated counterattack and called in part of the 5th Guards Mechanized Corps to assist. The 33rd Army crossed the Oder and attacked the town of Fürstenburg, while the 3rd Army of the 1st Byelorussian Front linked up with Koniev's 28th Army at Teupitz, thus completing the encirclement of the 9th Army. The 5th Guards Army also managed to halt Schörner's disruptive offensive towards Spremberg, although several days of hard fighting would be needed before the Germans were forced to withdraw.

25 APRIL 1945

The Army Group Vistula commander, GenObst Heinrici, visited von Manteuffel, whose 3rd Panzer Army was straining to hold 2nd Byelorussian Front on the Oder. He then moved on to the 25th Panzergrenadier Division where he found GenObst Jodl trying to convince Steiner to launch a counterattack to relieve Berlin. Both Jodl and Keitel were concerned with trying to relieve the city and rescue Hitler, but the field commanders were well aware that they just did not have the resources available and that the German Army in the east was crumbling rapidly. Heinrici soon learnt that the Soviets had broken through von Manteuffel's lines south of Stettin and authorized him to retreat according to a plan worked out previously. He then sent a message to OKW which Keitel finally received some 48 hours later.

About the only good news for Heinrici was that Obst Biehler's Frankfurt-an-der-Oder garrison had finally linked up with the 9th Army who were preparing to break out to the west, preceded by simultaneous breakouts by battlegroups led by Staf Rüdiger Pipkorn (the remnants of the 35th SS Police Grenadier and 10th SS 'Frundsberg' Panzer Divisions) and Obst Hans von Luck (the 125th Panzergrenadier Regiment). Both battlegroups managed to join up but were severely mauled on the way and the survivors retreated to rejoin the main group. Elsewhere, the day saw the historic link up between the Soviet 58th Guards Rifle Division and the American 69th Infantry Division near Torgau on the River Elbe that meant that Germany was now split in two.

Weidling issued his revised defence sector command organization, based on the deployment of the LVI Panzer Corps, but these commands were not as clear-cut as they appeared, the main problem being the relationship between the Waffen SS and Wehrmacht, which while usually 'workable' on the ground, often degenerated further up the chain of command. While ObstLt Seifert was in nominal command of the 'Zitadelle' sector and had a variety of troops under his command, SS-Brigaf Mohnke was directly responsible to Hitler for the defence of the Central Government Area including the Reichs Chancellery and buildings around it. His command consisted of various Waffen SS formations including the SS 'Anhalt' Regiments and Commander Kuhlmann's 'Grossadmiral Dönitz' Battalion, although he did not consider himself to be answerable to Weidling. Later in the day, SS-Brigaf Krukenberg was instructed to take over command of the 11th SS 'Nordland' Panzergrenadier Division from Ziegler, whom Weidling considered as a spent force.

The anticipated meeting between the 47th Army and 4th Guards Tank Army took place that morning near Ketzin while the 125th Rifle Corps continued its attacks on Spandau and Gatow Airfield. They succeeded in isolating the defenders in Spandau (under SS-Ogruf August Heissmeyer) but failed to dislodge those defending Gatow. The 2nd Guards Tank Army struggled to clear the industrial suburb of Siemensstadt due to a shortage of infantry. The 3rd Shock Army crossed the Hohenzollern Canal at the Plötzensee Locks (79th Rifle Corps) and took the prison after a hard fight, but could not advance any further without support due to the Königsdamm Bridge being blown and the area being under the full view of the German defenders across the canal. It also continued to advance into the Moabit area (12th Guards Rifle Corps) and fought its way (7th Rifle Corps) to the edge of Alexanderplatz.

Elsewhere, the 5th Shock Army advanced steadily towards the city centre, with the 26th Guards Rifle Corps advancing down either side of the Frankfurter Allee towards the Friedrichshain Flak Tower, the 32nd Rifle Corps coming up against the strong German defences around the Schlesischer Railway Station while the 9th Rifle Corps had forced the Landwehr Canal and become involved in heavy fighting around Görlitzer Railway Station. The 8th Guards Army (along with the 1st Guards Tank Army) forced the Teltow Canal with Tempelhof Airport as its objective. The airfield was defended by a strong flak unit with guns readily convertible into an anti-tank role, as well as miscellaneous support units. The 28th Guards Rifle Corps attacked the airfield directly (supported by two tank brigades) and had 29th Guards Rifle Corps (supported by 8th Guards Mechanized Corps) on its left and 4th Guards Rifle Corps on its right, supported by the 11th Guards Tank Corps. The 29th was held up by fierce German resistance at the airfield but the other two corps managed to cross the Teltow Canal and advance with little trouble. The 3rd Guards Tank Army (with elements of the 28th Army) faced stiff opposition as they

German four-barrelled 20mm Flak gun. While designed to engage low flying aircraft, such weapons proved to be useful in ground fighting, especially against infantry and lightly armoured vehicles. (Nik Cornish Library)

A Soviet soldier hurriedly makes his way from cover to cover in the centre of Berlin. This form of warfare was very infantry-intensive and strongly favoured the defence, who could snipe and spring ambushes on the attacking Soviets, quickly disappearing into the ruins during the confusion. (Topfoto/Novosti)

advanced towards the S-Bahn ring, added to which they were having to develop the tactics necessary for fighting in, first, the suburbs of south Berlin, and then the more densely built up areas of the central district, almost on the move. It would be a costly lesson in both material and men, just as it was in other formations. It was clear that the army was being moved in a northeasterly direction towards the Reichstag as Koniev wanted to beat Zhukov to the prize. The difficulties in aircraft coordination were also becoming apparent with a number of instances occurring due to the congested battlefield. Therefore Stavka changed the inter-Front boundary to run along the line of Mittenwalde, Tempelhof (the Goods Station) and Potsdamer Railway Station.

In Berchtesgaden, GenObst Ritter von Greim visited Gen Koller to discuss the situation. While he didn't share Koller's view on Göring's innocence regarding the events of 23 April, he agreed to deliver Koller's plea of mitigation to the Führer directly and, with Hanna Reisch, planned to make the dangerous trip to Berlin. Just before midnight, Jodl received Hitler's detailed instructions supplementing OKW's plans to relieve Berlin and stabilize the Eastern Front. They were wildly ambitious and completely ignored the true situation on the ground. Heinrici and his army commanders were well aware of what was really happening and covertly working on getting as many men over the Elbe as possible while fending off the Soviets. Hitler also authorized the formation of the 21st Army under Gen d.Inf Kurt von Tippelskirch to counter the possible thrust by the British 21st Army Group towards Lübeck that would cut off the province of Schleswig-Holstein and Denmark. As Steiner was awaiting reinforcements to conduct his relief effort (25th Panzergrenadier, 7th Panzer and 3rd Naval Divisions), the 3rd Panzer Army was forced to withdraw from the north–south line of the Uecker River running through Prenzlau due to continued Soviet pressure. In these circumstances, Steiner's attack would have been suicidal and Heinrici asked Jodl for the three divisions in order to stabilize von Manteuffel's front. Jodl refused and so Heinrici secretly put an embargo on the 7th Panzer Division.

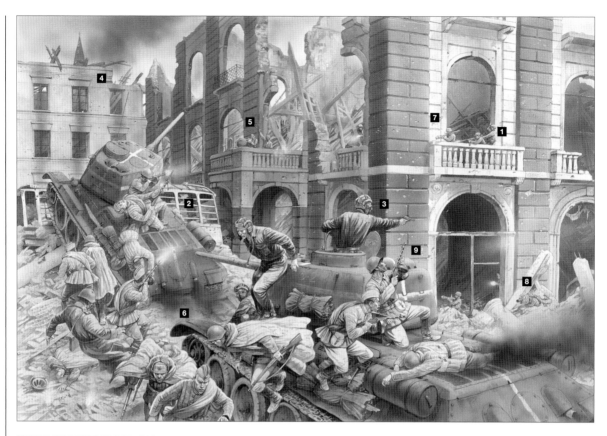

URBAN WARFARE IN BERLIN (pages 58–59)

The first Soviet troops to cross the city boundary were the 1st Mechanised and 12th Guards Tank Corps of the 2nd Guards Tank Army, which was acting as the vanguard for the 3rd and 5th Shock Armies. They entered the suburbs of Weissensee and Hohenschönhausen on the 21 April 1945. Shortly after that, began the revenge for the Germans' treatment of civilians and property in the Soviet Union, something that many Soviet troops had hungered for since Kursk. Looting, rape and (occasionally) murder were the order of the day in many places, and while this had originally been sanctioned by those in command, aware that this was not good for the image of communism, the Soviet authorities tried to reign in their forces. The Soviets faced a German defence that had already been prepared according to a plan by the former Berlin Defence Area Commandant, General Helmuth Reymann, and which was now to be bolstered by the arrival of the LVI Panzer Corps under General Weidling, although there was already a wide variety of Wehrmacht, Waffen SS, Volkssturm and Hitler Youth (1) units available. Cooperation, indeed coordination among these disparate units was often difficult at best, but the suspicion, if not hostility, between the Wehrmacht and the Waffen SS did little to improve matters. The Soviets found that they had to quickly change from manoeuvre warfare tactics to urban warfare tactics, without the benefit proper training. Hard lessons were learned, as it took time for the infantry, armour and artillery to establish the necessary tactics and coordination to work effectively together (2). It was difficult for tank crews (3), as they advanced into built-up areas (4), to see where the enemy had concealed himself (particularly if he was in the cellar of a building) or had constructed fortifications (5). Tanks proceeding in column (6) were excellent targets for small teams armed with Panzerfausts (7) or Panzerschreks (8), who would knock out the first and last tanks, especially when they had been stopped by barricades constructed by local volunteers. They then attempted to create enough confusion to keep the infantry's (9) heads down and then, if possible, proceeded to destroy the remaining tanks one-by-one before slipping away. It was important, therefore, that the tanks, infantry, artillery and engineers cooperated effectively to eliminate the defenders as quickly as possible. The forces from the various arms were generally organized into Combat Teams generally consisting of a platoon of infantry, two or three tanks or self-propelled guns, some sappers and some heavy weapons, such as flamethrowers or even artillery pieces, although the gun crews were vulnerable to enemy fire, as were the forward observers. (Peter Dennis)

26 APRIL 1945

At dawn, Wenck launched his relief attack, led by the XX Corps from the line of Brandenberg–Belzig towards Potsdam. The roads were blocked with refugees so the troops moved across country and caught the 6th Guards Mechanized Corps in an exposed flank, capturing whole units intact as well as a German Field Hospital with staff, medical supplies and over 3,000 patients. The young soldiers fought with all the élan of the Wehrmacht during the early years of the war and covered 11 miles on the first day.

The 79th Rifle Corps continued with its efforts to get over the Westhafen Canal and finally succeeded with the help of direct artillery support and a smoke screen, although the strongpoint at the Beusselstrasse S-Bahn Station continued to hold out. Heavy fighting continued to occupy the 5th Shock Army, with only the 9th Rifle Corps making any progress as it cleared the Görlitzer Railway Station, and pushed forward into Kreuzberg. Chuikov's forces, having taken the airport at Tempelhof, continued to move towards the Landwehr Canal while gradually wheeling left, their right flank moving up the canal. By the end of the day the 8th Guards Army and 1st Guards Tank Army were up to Potsdamer Strasse on the left and Heinrich-von-Kleist Park in the centre, beyond the inter-front boundary established by Stavka and in the line of advance for the 3rd Guards Tank Army.

Weidling was informed that ObstLt Erich Bärenfanger (a previous Defence Commandant) had been reinstated as the commander of defence sectors A and B and promoted. While this was due to successful wire-pulling on Bärenfanger's part, it suited Weidling, who had moved his headquarters from the Hohenzollerndamm, first to the cellars of the old OKH buildings on Bendlerstrasse, then to the Army Signals Bunker

A Soviet Katyusha Multiple-Rocket Launcher in a Berlin street. These vehicles, called 'Stalin Organs' by the Germans, could carry up to 48 rockets with the most common being 82mm or 132mm in size. (From the fonds of the RGAKFD at Krasnogorsk)

INTO THE CENTRE OF BERLIN
SOVIET OPERATIONS 28 APRIL – 2 MAY 1945

Soviet forces established bridgeheads but impromptu urban warfare, road blocks and German tank-hunting teams continued to extract a heavy toll.

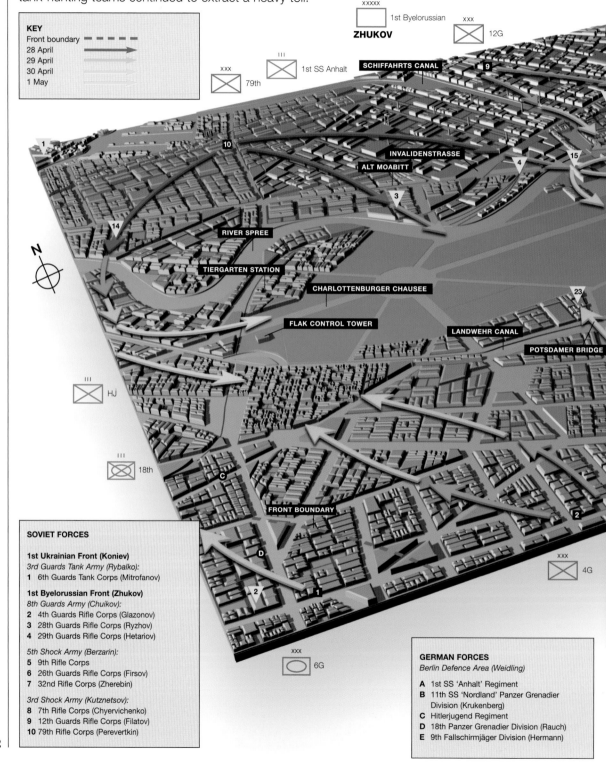

KEY

Front boundary
28 April
29 April
30 April
1 May

XXXXX
ZHUKOV
1st Byelorussian

XXX
12G

XXX
79th

III
1st SS Anhalt

SCHIFFAHRTS CANAL

9

INVALIDENSTRASSE

ALT MOABITT

4

15

3

14

23

RIVER SPREE

TIERGARTEN STATION

CHARLOTTENBURGER CHAUSEE

LANDWEHR CANAL

FLAK CONTROL TOWER

POTSDAMER BRIDGE

III
HJ

III
18th

C

FRONT BOUNDARY

2

D

XXX
4G

2

1

XXX
6G

SOVIET FORCES

1st Ukrainian Front (Koniev)
3rd Guards Tank Army (Rybalko):
1 6th Guards Tank Corps (Mitrofanov)

1st Byelorussian Front (Zhukov)
8th Guards Army (Chuikov):
2 4th Guards Rifle Corps (Glazonov)
3 28th Guards Rifle Corps (Ryzhov)
4 29th Guards Rifle Corps (Hetariov)

5th Shock Army (Berzarin):
5 9th Rifle Corps
6 26th Guards Rifle Corps (Firsov)
7 32nd Rifle Corps (Zherebin)

3rd Shock Army (Kutznetsov):
8 7th Rifle Corps (Chyervichenko)
9 12th Guards Rifle Corps (Filatov)
10 79th Rifle Corps (Perevertkin)

GERMAN FORCES
Berlin Defence Area (Weidling)

A 1st SS 'Anhalt' Regiment
B 11th SS 'Nordland' Panzer Grenadier Division (Krukenberg)
C Hitlerjugend Regiment
D 18th Panzer Grenadier Division (Rauch)
E 9th Fallschirmjäger Division (Hermann)

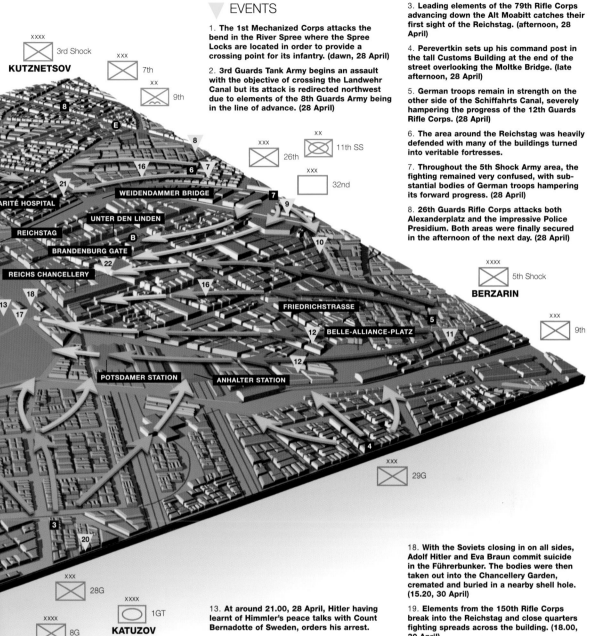

▼ EVENTS

1. The 1st Mechanized Corps attacks the bend in the River Spree where the Spree Locks are located in order to provide a crossing point for its infantry. (dawn, 28 April)

2. 3rd Guards Tank Army begins an assault with the objective of crossing the Landwehr Canal but its attack is redirected northwest due to elements of the 8th Guards Army being in the line of advance. (28 April)

3. Leading elements of the 79th Rifle Corps advancing down the Alt Moabitt catches their first sight of the Reichstag. (afternoon, 28 April)

4. Perevertkin sets up his command post in the tall Customs Building at the end of the street overlooking the Moltke Bridge. (late afternoon, 28 April)

5. German troops remain in strength on the other side of the Schiffahrts Canal, severely hampering the progress of the 12th Guards Rifle Corps. (28 April)

6. The area around the Reichstag was heavily defended with many of the buildings turned into veritable fortresses.

7. Throughout the 5th Shock Army area, the fighting remained very confused, with substantial bodies of German troops hampering its forward progress. (28 April)

8. 26th Guards Rifle Corps attacks both Alexanderplatz and the impressive Police Presidium. Both areas were finally secured in the afternoon of the next day. (28 April)

9. 32nd Rifle Corps only advanced very slowly as it was still busy reducing a number of German strongpoints including the Schlesische Railway Station.

10. 9th Rifle Corps managed to take the Spittelmarkt area early on as the area had been thoroughly reduced by artillery fire.

11. 301st Rifle Division takes the Reichs Patents Office on the Landwehr Canal embankment towards the end of the day. (evening, 28 April)

12. Continued Soviet attempts to move tanks up the Friedrichstrasse, Wilhelmstrasse and Saarlandstrasse are countered by German tank hunting teams.

13. At around 21.00, 28 April, Hitler having learnt of Himmler's peace talks with Count Bernadotte of Sweden, orders his arrest.

14. 12th Guards Tank Corps continues to advance through the western Moabitt but has to finally halt to due the depletion of its infantry support. (29 April)

15. The 79th Rifle Corps manages to establish a bridgehead on the other side of the Moltke Bridge from where it can secure the Diplomatic Quarter, Ministry of the Interior, Kroll Opera House. (morning, 29 April)

16. 5th Shock Army continued to make slow but steady progress as it encountered bitter German opposition, with strongpoints at the Börse S-Bahn Station, Rotes Rathaus, Christus Church and the Post Office Ministry.

17. Chuikov's 8th Guards Army started an assault directly across the Landwehr Canal and while several bridgeheads were established by the end of the day, the cost was enormous. (29 April)

18. With the Soviets closing in on all sides, Adolf Hitler and Eva Braun commit suicide in the Führerbunker. The bodies were then taken out into the Chancellery Garden, cremated and buried in a nearby shell hole. (15.20, 30 April)

19. Elements from the 150th Rifle Corps break into the Reichstag and close quarters fighting spreads across the building. (18.00, 30 April)

20. General Krebs, along with General Weidling's Chief of Staff, Colonel von Dufving, attempt to negotiate a ceasefire after making their way to Chuikov's headquarters. The initial offer is refused. (1 May)

21. Numerous breakout attempts begin, including one over the Weidendammer Bridge, a number of which are successful with both German troops and civilians making their way westwards. (1 – 2 May)

22. Soviet troops from the 9th Rifle Corps, 5th Shock Army storm the Reichs Chancellery. Major Anna Nikulina hoists the Red Flag from the roof. (morning, 2 May)

23. General Weidling (through his Chief of Staff, Colonel von Dufving) negotiates the surrender of the Berlin Garrison. (13.00, 2 May)

outside. Mummert could resume command of the 'Müncheberg' Panzer Division and it also released Obst Wöhlermann to take over command of the defence artillery. The 'Nord-West' Regiment fighting in Alexanderplatz was now down to below half-strength and was therefore disbanded, the survivors transferring to Bärenfanger's command. The 18th Panzergrenadier Division sent a battlegroup supported by six tanks and fifteen APCs to try and restore contact with the 20th Panzergrenadier Division but were beaten back by strong Soviet resistance. This led the 3rd Guards Tank Army to advance cautiously as it slowly adapted its techniques to the more built-up areas of Grunewald, Schmargendorf and Steglitz, although the 55th Guards Tank Brigade managed to make its way far enough to overrun an ammunition dump near the Teufelsee and stop in the Eichkamp area. Meanwhile, the pilot that had flown Speer into Berlin and back again flew Hanna Reisch and von Greim into Gatow in a Focke-Wulf 190 but no contact could be made with the Führerbunker. Von Greim and Reisch then continued in a Fieseler 'Storch' until von Greim was injured by anti-aircraft fire and Reisch had to conduct an emergency landing. They commandeered a passing vehicle and arrived at the bunker to learn that Hitler had merely wanted to confer on von Greim the command of the Luftwaffe with the rank of Generalfeldmarschall.

27 APRIL 1945

North of Berlin, von Manteuffel's 3rd Panzer Army had so far managed to contain the pressure from Rokossovsky's 2nd Byelorussian Front, but Soviet forces finally broke through just north of Prenzlau and OKW reluctantly assigned the 7th Panzer and 25th Panzergrenadier Divisions (on Heinrici's request) to help relieve the pressure and not participate in Steiner's attack, although they were to revert to their original task immediately the situation stabilized. Heinrici, however, had no intention of following this course of action and dug them in on the line Neubrandenburg–Neustrelitz to cover the main line of retreat. The 3rd Naval Division had also suffered during the 3rd Panzer Army's retreat and ceased to exist as a fighting force. To the west, Gatow and its airport finally fell and the Soviets were able to clear the west bank of the Havel opposite the city. The leading elements of the 47th Army reached Rathenow and Fehrbellin on their way to the Elbe but faced strong opposition from Holste's XXXXI Panzer Corps and so any further advance had to be delayed. In the meantime, to the south of the city, General Busse's 9th Army continued to try and break out of its pocket, but these attempts coincided with Soviet attacks to tighten the noose and they came to nothing, while Wenck's 12th Army reached the village of Ferch, just south of Potsdam.

In Berlin itself, continued pressure from Chuikov's 8th Guards Army had forced Krukenberg's 11th SS 'Nordland' Panzergrenadier Division to take up new positions across the Landwehr Canal, along the line of Spittelmarkt–Belle-Alliance-Platz, with the divisional command post in the cellars of the State Opera on the Unter den Linden. Krukenberg considered his unit to be directly under the control of Brigaf Mohnke and ignored the local defence sector commandant, ObstLt Seifert, who was encamped in the Air Ministry. Behind them lay the remains of the 'Müncheberg' Panzer Division.

Elements of the 2nd Guards Tank Army finished clearing the Siemensstadt and closed up on the banks of the River Spree from where it joined the Havel in the west to the Westhafen Canal in the east. Indeed, the 35th Mechanized Brigade had crossed the Spree in the area of Ruhleben despite most of the bridges having been destroyed. This coincided with a thrust along the Reichsstrasse by the 55th Guards Tank Brigade from 3rd Guards Tank Army that had been reinforced and were under orders to make for Ruhleben and link up with the 1st Byelorussian Front in order to seal off the garrison. Elements of the two brigades met near the Charlottenburger Chaussee and the 35th then withdrew back across the Spree, leaving the 55th to finish clearing the area. Weidling, however, could not afford to lose this potential escape route and so sent elements of the 18th Panzergrenadier Division to help the local defence, which meant that the Soviet forces there were insufficient to contain the Germans, who could infiltrate through their lines with ease.

The 79th Rifle Corps continued its advance down through Moabit and faced a bitter defence from a real mixed-bag of units, including a number of General Andrei Vlassov's White Russians, in a district whose heavy, solidly built buildings made the going slow and costly. However, a large number of Soviet prisoners of war were released from prisons in the area and so these were used to replenish losses. The remainder of the 3rd Shock Army faced a difficult task in reducing a number of strong-points (such as the Stettiner Railway Station), supported by the Humboldthain Flak Tower, and street fighting continued with the 9th Fallschirmjäger Division exacting a heavy toll amongst the chaos and confusion. Despite the willingness of the higher command to continue the advance during the night, the situation on the ground meant that the frontline units usually used the hours of darkness to rest, reorganize, replenish supplies and replace losses. The street-fighting techniques of the 1st Byelorussian Front consisted of assigning a street to a complete rifle regiment, with one battalion on each side and a third bringing up the rear, while the supporting artillery moved through the backyards with the help of engineers.

The 5th Shock Army made little progress as the whole of that area was in a chaotic state with fighting going on everywhere, especially around strongpoints such as the Lowen—Bohnisch Brewery, Schlesischer Railway Station and Friedrichshain Flak Tower. The 8th Guards Army moved up to the line of the Landwehr Canal and consolidated their positions, although there were still pockets of German resistance and Chuikov established his command post in a house at No. 2 Schulenburgring. Along with the 3rd Shock Army advancing south across the Spree, and 5th Shock Army advancing west through the city centre, Chuikov was responsible for clearing the southern part of the Tiergarten, including the Potsdamer and Anhalter Railway Stations. The 3rd Guards Tank Army continued its attack up the Hohenzollerndamm and Avus motorway but were blocked by the 30th Panzergrenadier Regiment and elements of the 118th Panzer Regiment, while the 51st Panzergrenadier Regiment fought a delaying action in Schöneberg. However, Soviet pressure forced the division to withdraw to the inner defence ring along the S-Bahn between the Westend and Schmargendorf Stations. The 55th Guards Tank Brigade managed to advance all the way to the hill containing the Olympic Stadium and Reichs Sports Academy, which was under the jurisdiction of Obst Anton Eder and his Defence Sector 'F', but were driven back by a local counterattack.

28 APRIL 1945

During the early hours, Keitel, who was unaware of what was happening on the 3rd Panzer Army's front, visited Steiner who could give him no information on the whereabouts of the 7th Panzer Division. Keitel then promised him the 'Schlageter' RAD Infantry Division as a replacement but this formation had ceased to exist as an effective fighting force a week earlier. Steiner assured Keitel that he was preparing to mount a relief effort, but secretly had no intention of committing his men to an effort with so little chance of success. Hitler meanwhile had grown tired of Steiner's procrastination and ordered GenLt Holste of the XXXXI Panzer Corps to take over the effort. Holste asked for time to prepare for the attack as he had to manoeuvre his troops into position and deal with the 47th Army. On his way back to OKW, Keitel discovered what had happened to the two divisions sent to help Heinrici and that the 3rd Panzer Army was actually in full retreat in contravention of Hitler's orders and without consulting OKW. Jodl and Keitel confronted both Heinrici and von Manteuffel at the crossroads west of Neubrandenburg about what was happening but were faced down after an angry exchange.

During the evening, Busse had incorporated the survivors of the Frankfurt-an-der-Oder garrison and prepared to break out. The point of attack would be near Halbe, as this was the Soviet inter-front boundary where coordination would be weakest. Once through, they faced a journey through almost 40 miles of woodland that would serve to hinder Soviet aircraft and artillery. The XI SS Panzer Corps would effect the breakthrough and then cover the northern flank, followed by the V Corps who would take over the lead and cover the southern flank with the V SS Mountain Corps (along with the 21st Panzer Division) covering the rear of the retreat. The breakout started as soon as dusk fell and thousands of refugees moved with the troops. The XI SS Panzer Corps broke through the Soviet lines and the main body of the 9th Army moved through, although elements of the rearguard became entangled with the Soviet attempts to close the breach and an intense struggle developed.

While the leading elements of 125th Rifle Corps had secured Gatow and started to attack Potsdam from the north, the 20,000-strong garrison under Gen Reymann had made contact with Wenck's 12th Army and began to withdraw along the lakeside or by using inflatable boats. After vacating Ruhleben, the 2nd Guards Tank Army redeployed to attack across the Spree Locks directly north of the Schloss Charlottenburg gardens and the Jungfernheide S-Bahn Station strongpoint (1st Mechanized Corps) and south towards the Landwehr Canal adjacent to the Moabit area (12th Guards Tank Corps). In the 3rd Shock Army sector, the 79th Rifle Corps continued its advance down the Alt Moabit and caught sight of the Reichstag. The closeness of their ultimate objective would lead to sacrifice of heroic proportions and highlight the ruthlessness by which the higher level commanders exploited their troops to meet a politically dictated deadline, for the pressure from Stalin was such that no one wanted to be

BREAKOUT OF THE 9TH ARMY, 28 APRIL–1 MAY 1945

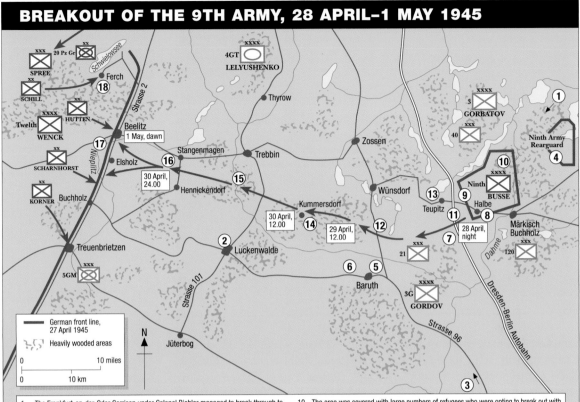

1. The Frankfurt-an-der-Oder Garrison under Colonel Biehler managed to break through to the 9th Army, trapped in the vicinity of Halbe (25 April).
2. Busse quickly organized his troops for a breakout to the west. They were to be spearheaded by Colonel Hans von Luck's battlegroup, who were to attack west over the Dresden–Berlin Autobahn.
3. At the same time, a battlegroup led by SS Colonel Rudiger Pipkorn, was to move westward from Schrepzig, north of Lübben.
4. The remainder of the force consisted of XI SS Panzer Corps, V Corps and V SS Mountain Corps who were to act as rearguard.
5. Von Luck's battlegroup started its attack and by midnight had reached the northern outskirts of Baruth (20.00, 25 April).
6. The Pipkorn battlegroup managed to break out and the two groups joined up. They once again tried to advance west with only limited success.
7. The 9th Army continued its attempts to break out during the 26th and 27th, but they coincided with the Soviets trying to tighten the noose and casualties on both sides were heavy.
8. With General Wenck's attack diverting Soviet attention away from them, General Busse prepared once again to break through their lines in the guise of joining forces with Wenck and driving towards Berlin (28 / 29 April).
9. The 9th Army was organized as before for the breakout except the 21st Panzer Division was to cover the breakout from the northwest.

10. The area was covered with large numbers of refugees who were opting to break out with the troops, however slim their chances were.
11. The XI SS Panzer Corps started its assault as soon as dusk settled, finally breaking through with the main body of the 9th Army following (28 April).
12. The 9th Army reached the Soviet blocking position on the Zossen–Baruth road by midday on the 29th, breaking through by the early evening.
13. The V SS Mountain Corps and 21st Panzer Division failed to break through the Soviet cordon and were destroyed in an intense battle which inflicted severe casualties and diverted attention away from the rest of the 9th Army (30 April).
14. The 9th Army reached Kummersdorf by midday where they rested briefly. The rest of the day was spent moving northwest then west towards Hennickendorf (30 April).
15. After breaking through another Soviet cordon, they were shelled and bombed by aircraft and faced numerous Soviet attacks and deception attempts by German troops fighting for the Soviets, the so-called 'Seydlitz Troops' (30 April).
16. After reaching Hennickendorf, the 9th Army had to fight through positions held by the 5th Guards Mechanized Corps in the early morning darkness (a.m., 1 May).
17. The exhausted survivors of the 9th Army reached the positions of Wenck's 12th Army south of Beelitz. (dawn, 1 May).
18. The 'Spree' Army Detachment and 20th Panzer Grenadier Division took advantage of Wenck's advance to just south of Potsdam and withdrew through his lines.

accused of sabotaging the project. The cost was of no consequence. The 79th Rifle Corps would face a tremendously challenging task as the only crossing still standing was the heavily barricaded and mined Moltke Bridge that was in full view of the German strongpoints across the river in the Ministry of the Interior and the Diplomatic Quarter. Beyond these lay additional strongpoints, emplacements, trenches, fortifications, gun positions and water obstacles right up to the Reichstag itself. Fortunately, the losses incurred in fighting through Moabit had been replaced by freed prisoners of war, bringing most battalions up to their establishment strength of 500 men in three rifle companies, a support weapons company and a battery of 45mm field guns.

The 5th Shock Army continued to make steady progress, although the fighting continued to be very confused with German strongpoints continuing to hold out in the Friedrichshain Flak Tower, Landsberger Chaussee and Frankfurter Allee area. The 26th Guards Rifle Corps

attacked Alexanderplatz and the Police Presidium, while the 32nd Rifle Corps was still trying to reduce the Schlesischer Railway Station. The 9th Rifle Corps took the Spittelmarkt and Reichs Patent Office against determined opposition and was now only some 1,500 yards from their goal – the Reichs Chancellery. The 8th Guards Army continued its preparations to move across the Landwehr Canal and deployed the maximum number of artillery pieces and rocket launchers in a direct fire role. The individual assault groups would be left to their own devices as to how to cross the canal but Chuikov reserved for himself the operation to cross the still intact Potsdamer Bridge, as the whole area was heavily defended and swept by enfilade fire. The 3rd Guards Tank Army launched an attack to cross the Landwehr Canal but found that elements of Chuikov's 8th Guards Army had already occupied positions on the line of advance and so the attack was redirected northwest after the 9th Mechanized Corps was redeployed to the left flank. This was a relief for the 56th Guards Tank Brigade as it had attracted the full attention of the German tank-hunting teams based around Fehrbelliner Platz where the 51st Panzergrenadier Regiment was holding out.

Late in the evening, the news of Himmler's peace talks with Count Bernadotte of Sweden reached Hitler who flew into yet another rage. He ordered von Greim to use all the remaining Luftwaffe assets to help with the defence of Berlin, to find Himmler and bring him to justice. At this stage of the conflict, Hitler could have little impact on events, which were very much in the hands of the field commanders. Even Weidling himself could do little to influence things – he had taken command too late to influence the defence plans and had few reserves to speak of. He did not even have the freedom of action of others like Heinrici, von Manteuffel, Busse and Wencke, as there were just too many fanatical Nazis wanting to fight to the bitter end. Hitler then announced his intention to marry his mistress, Eva Braun, and then began dictating his personal and political statements to one of his secretaries, Traudl Junge,

Soviet infantry moving down a Berlin street. Infantry out in the open like this were especially vulnerable to ambushes and sniping. Given their disposition, something has just caught these soldiers' attention further down the street. (Central Museum of the Armed Forces, Moscow)

naming Dönitz as his successor to the Presidency and Göbbels as Chancellor. Elsewhere, von Manteuffel telephoned Heinrici to say that the 3rd Panzer Army was now in full retreat and that Jodl be invited to see the situation for himself. Heinrici passed this information on to Keitel who accused him of flagrant disobedience to which Heinrici retorted that he could not accept the responsibility of commanding troops under the impossible conditions imposed by OKW. Keitel then relieved him of command.

29 APRIL 1945

It was becoming increasingly difficult for Wenck's 12th Army to hold their extended line against increasing Soviet pressure as they awaited the arrival of Busse's 9th Army. As the predicament grew more serious, it became clear that Wenck would not be able to continue the advance towards Berlin and therefore sent a signal to Weidling informing him of this. It is unclear whether or not Weidling received it, as there was no acknowledgement. The 9th Army managed to break through the Soviet lines between Zossen and Baruth and then rested briefly just west of the road before continuing their trek westwards. Some of the rearguard, that included elements of the V SS Mountain Corps and 21st Panzer Division as well as a large number of civilians, had failed to escape the Soviet encirclement and were in the process of being wiped out. The ensuing fighting, however, was so intense that the Soviets themselves suffered heavy casualties and so were misled into believing that they had caught the majority of the 9th Army and so failed to pursue the remainder.

Busse signalled Wenck to indicate that while there was still a good chance that the army would reach him, it was virtually finished as an

ASSAULT ON THE REICHSTAG
SOVIET OPERATIONS 28 APRIL – 2 MAY 1945

As Soviet troops catch their first glimpse of the Reichstag, victory appears to be in their grasp, but their opponents do not know the meaning of defeat.

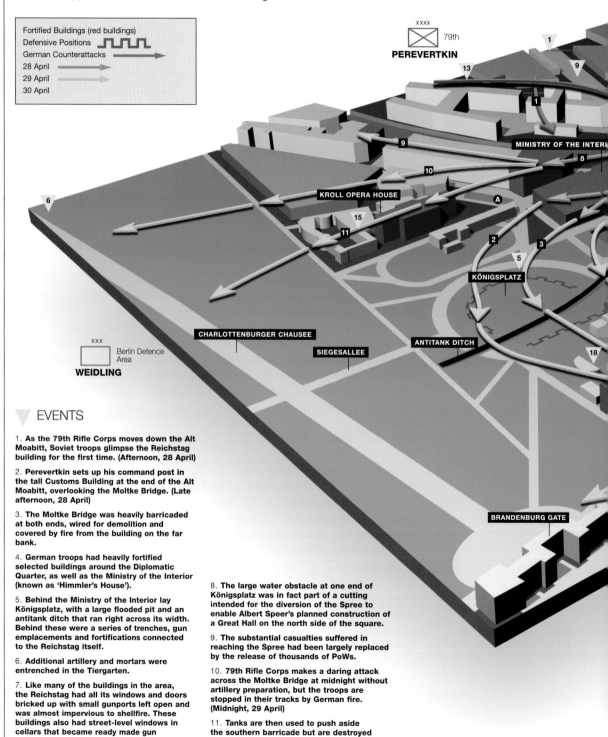

Fortified Buildings (red buildings)
Defensive Positions
German Counterattacks
28 April
29 April
30 April

XXXX
79th
PEREVERTKIN

MINISTRY OF THE INTERI

KROLL OPERA HOUSE

A

KÖNIGSPLATZ

CHARLOTTENBURGER CHAUSEE

SIEGESALLEE

ANTITANK DITCH

XXX
Berlin Defence Area
WEIDLING

BRANDENBURG GATE

▼ EVENTS

1. As the 79th Rifle Corps moves down the Alt Moabitt, Soviet troops glimpse the Reichstag building for the first time. (Afternoon, 28 April)

2. Perevertkin sets up his command post in the tall Customs Building at the end of the Alt Moabitt, overlooking the Moltke Bridge. (Late afternoon, 28 April)

3. The Moltke Bridge was heavily barricaded at both ends, wired for demolition and covered by fire from the building on the far bank.

4. German troops had heavily fortified selected buildings around the Diplomatic Quarter, as well as the Ministry of the Interior (known as 'Himmler's House').

5. Behind the Ministry of the Interior lay Königsplatz, with a large flooded pit and an antitank ditch that ran right across its width. Behind these were a series of trenches, gun emplacements and fortifications connected to the Reichstag itself.

6. Additional artillery and mortars were entrenched in the Tiergarten.

7. Like many of the buildings in the area, the Reichstag had all its windows and doors bricked up with small gunports left open and was almost impervious to shellfire. These buildings also had street-level windows in cellars that became ready made gun embrasures.

8. The large water obstacle at one end of Königsplatz was in fact part of a cutting intended for the diversion of the Spree to enable Albert Speer's planned construction of a Great Hall on the north side of the square.

9. The substantial casualties suffered in reaching the Spree had been largely replaced by the release of thousands of PoWs.

10. 79th Rifle Corps makes a daring attack across the Moltke Bridge at midnight without artillery preparation, but the troops are stopped in their tracks by German fire. (Midnight, 29 April)

11. Tanks are then used to push aside the southern barricade but are destroyed by antitank gun fire.

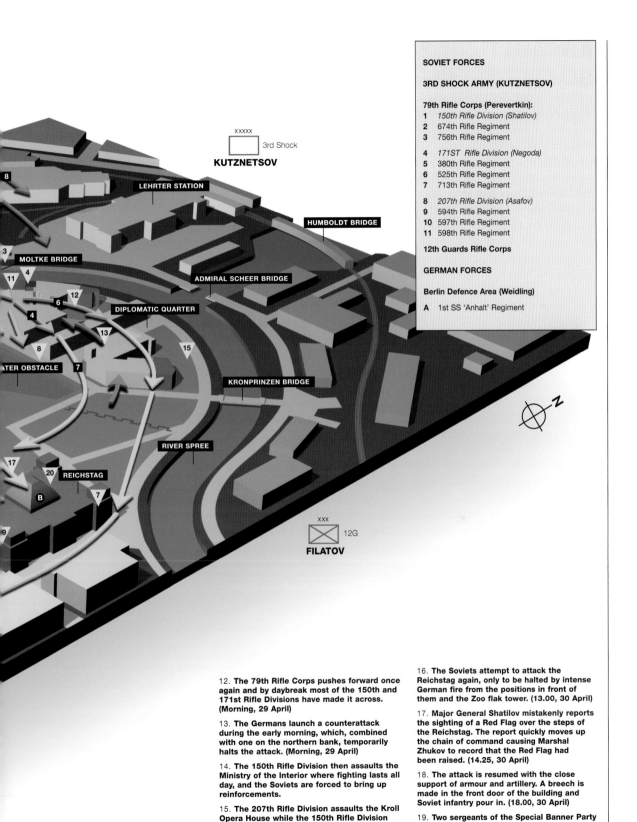

8

XXXXX
3rd Shock
KUTZNETSOV

LEHRTER STATION

HUMBOLDT BRIDGE

3

MOLTKE BRIDGE

4

11

12

6

4

13

8

15

ADMIRAL SCHEER BRIDGE

DIPLOMATIC QUARTER

ITER OBSTACLE

7

KRONPRINZEN BRIDGE

17

20

REICHSTAG

B

7

RIVER SPREE

9

N

XXX
12G
FILATOV

12. The 79th Rifle Corps pushes forward once again and by daybreak most of the 150th and 171st Rifle Divisions have made it across. (Morning, 29 April)

13. The Germans launch a counterattack during the early morning, which, combined with one on the northern bank, temporarily halts the attack. (Morning, 29 April)

14. The 150th Rifle Division then assaults the Ministry of the Interior where fighting lasts all day, and the Soviets are forced to bring up reinforcements.

15. The 207th Rifle Division assaults the Kroll Opera House while the 150th Rifle Division moves across Königsplatz only to be halted at the water-filled antitank ditch and the 171st Rifle Division continues to clear the eastern half of the Diplomatic Quarter. (Morning, 30 April)

16. The Soviets attempt to attack the Reichstag again, only to be halted by intense German fire from the positions in front of them and the Zoo flak tower. (13.00, 30 April)

17. Major General Shatilov mistakenly reports the sighting of a Red Flag over the steps of the Reichstag. The report quickly moves up the chain of command causing Marshal Zhukov to record that the Red Flag had been raised. (14.25, 30 April)

18. The attack is resumed with the close support of armour and artillery. A breech is made in the front door of the building and Soviet infantry pour in. (18.00, 30 April)

19. Two sergeants of the Special Banner Party manage to reach the roof and succeed in wedging Red Banner No. 5 into a convenient crevice. The two sergeants in question are made 'Heroes of the Soviet Union'. (22.50, 30 April)

effective fighting force and Wenck therefore passed this information on to OKW, who had already decided that 12th Army itself was too weak to effect a relief of the city. OKW reluctantly acknowledged and so Wenck was free to pursue his own plan.

Meanwhile, von Manteuffel had been ordered to take over command of Army Group Vistula after the dismissal of Heinrici, but von Manteuffel, who was loyal to both his former commander and the troops directly under him, refused, citing the imminent crisis facing the 3rd Panzer Army as the reason he could not take up the appointment. OKW then decided to appoint GenObst Kurt Student as the new army group commander and fly him back from Holland, but in the meantime, Gen von Tippelskirch, in charge of the newly forming 21st Army, would take command, much to his reluctance. The 2nd Byelorussian Front was pressing hard and had taken Anklam in the north, Neubrandenburg and Neustrelitz in the centre and crossed the Havel on its southern flank, while the British 21st Army Group had taken Lauenburg, where FM Ernst Busch was struggling to keep open the gap near Lübeck. With Soviet ground forces close to their location, OKW sent one last transmission to Hitler in the Führerbunker and then moved out, joining 3rd Panzer Army in its general retreat.

During the day, a number of parties left the bunker, including two couriers who were tasked with taking Hitler's personal and political statements to Grossadmiral Dönitz. For this task, Bormann selected his personal adviser, SS Standartenführer Wilhelm Zander, along with Heinz Lorenz of the Propaganda Ministry. A third set would be sent to GFM Schörner in the care of Hitler's aide-de-camp, Maj Willi Johannmeier.

During the morning, the 2nd Guards Tank Army's sector saw a breakthrough across the Spree locks by the 1st Mechanized Corps and through the Jungfernheide S-Bahn Station position by the 219th Tank Brigade. The 12th Guards Tank Corps continued to make steady progress in the western Moabit but the army was now desperately short of infantry and Zhukov had to send the 1st Polish Infantry Division as there were no Soviet reinforcements immediately available. The 79th Rifle Corps attacked across the Moltke Bridge after preparations had gone on during the previous night. Soviet tanks had pushed aside the northern barricade on the bridge whilst the Germans had reinforced their forces holding the Ministry of the Interior and the buildings immediately around it. In the early hours, the two leading battalions launched a surprise attack across the bridge, reinforced with heavy tanks, but were beaten back by heavy fire. A second attack managed to establish a small bridgehead in one corner of the Diplomatic Quarter, which the Soviets sought to expand as the day wore on and the fighting spread across the area. The Soviets eventually managed to force their way into the Ministry of the Interior (nicknamed 'Himmler's House') and along the Herwarthstrasse. The 'Anhalt' Regiment then mounted a counterattack, which, along with a group of paratroopers from the 9th Fallschirmjäger Division who broke through the Soviet lines to cross the bridge and join the defence, held up the Soviet advance.

The 3rd Shock Army continued to make slow progress against determined opposition, particularly from the German strongpoint at the Stettiner Railway Station. The same was true for the 5th Shock Army, as the 26th Guards Rifle Corps gradually made its way towards the Börse (Stock Exchange) S-Bahn Station and Rotes Rathaus (Red Townhall), while clearing Alexanderplatz. The Rathaus was defended by elements of the 11th SS 'Nordlund' Panzergrenadier Division and the Soviets had to fight for the building room-by-room. The 32nd Rifle Corps managed to take the Jannowitzbrücke S-Bahn Station and closed up to the Spree, which it prepared to cross. Finally, the 9th Rifle Corps, supported by the 92nd Guards Tank Regiment, moved up Saarlandstrasse towards the Anhalter Railway Station but encountered German strongpoints at the Christus Church and Post Office building on Möckernstrasse. The 8th Guards Army began its assault across the Landwehr Canal, preceded by a powerful artillery barrage. Even so, progress was slow and casualties were very high, but by the end of the day the Soviets had managed to gain a number of footholds and were across the Potsdamer Bridge. The 3rd Guards Tank Army continued its reduction of Wilmersdorf but encountered confusion with the change to the inter-front boundary, whereupon it was forced to withdraw its 55th Tank Brigade from what was now 2nd Guards Tank Army territory.

That evening, Hitler sent requests for information to Brigaf Mohnke as to where the Soviets had reached in Berlin and to OKW as to the progress of the relief effort. Mohnke replied that the Soviets had virtually reached the Weidendammer Bridge in the north, were in the Lustgarten and the Air Ministry to the east, in Potsdamer Strasse to the south and in the Tiergarten to the west, perhaps some 400 yards away. Keitel's reply was surprisingly honest and basically stated that the 12th Army had reached Potsdam but were fighting off Soviet attacks and could not now continue their advance on Berlin, while the 9th Army had managed to break out but its location was unknown, as was its strength. The situation was therefore hopeless and Hitler decided that suicide was the only option.

The body of a dead German soldier rests on the steps of the Reichs Chancellery, May 1945. It is unclear as to whether he lies where he fell or was placed there in order to have a 'posed' shot. The Soviets assaulted the Chancellery on 2 May 1945 but encountered only light resistance, most of the defenders having withdrawn. (Topfoto/Topham)

30 APRIL 1945

During the morning, Hitler again consulted with Mohnke who stated that the Soviets were gradually making their way ever closer and could be expected to mount a major assault on the Chancellery the next day, which was May Day. Hitler then gave permission for the troops to undertake a breakout, an order that was passed to Weidling who instructed his staff to plan for a breakout later that night. None of the Waffen SS attended the conference, considering it a matter for Weidling and the rest of the garrison.

The 79th Rifle Corps had managed to clear the Ministry of the Interior (150th Rifle Division) and the western half of the Diplomatic Quarter (171st Rifle Division) of defenders, but there was to be no respite. Stalin was determined that his exhausted soldiers would take the Reichstag and so the 207th Rifle Division advanced south

THE ATTTACK ON THE REICHSTAG (pages 74–75)

The 79th Rifle Corps had first spotted the Reichstag building as it had advanced down the Alt Moabitt on the afternoon of the 28 April. The Corps however faced an extremely tough time moving across the Moltke Bridge and had to clear German strongpoints in the Ministry of the Interior, Kroll Opera House and Diplomatic Quarter before attempting an assault on the Reichstag itself on 30 April. After three early attempts had been thwarted, and a mistaken message sent out that a red flag had been seen over the steps of the Reichstag near the right-hand column, the 79th Rifle Corps' attack was resumed at 18.00 and this time, with the close support of armour and self-propelled artillery, Soviet infantry from the 380th, 674th and 756th Rifle Regiments managed to make it up the steps of the Reichstag and to blast a small hole in the bricked up doorway, making their way into the main entrance hall. As more and more Soviet infantry entered (1), vicious hand-to-hand fighting spread throughout the floors of the building. The Germans put up a very stubborn resistance (2) and used the layout of the building as well as the twilight conditions to their advantage (3). The Soviets experienced great difficulty in picking their way through the rubble, especially in the remains of the 'Hall of the Diet', strewn with rubble and debris (4). Here, Soviet infantry tried time and again to advance across the chamber (5) with the support of comrades in the balconies behind them (6), but were stopped by Waffen SS defenders barricaded on the opposite side (7). In such close-quarter fighting, pistols, grenades and sub-machineguns were the best weapons. The Soviets were armed with the PPSh-41 sub-machinegun (8), Nagant revolver and Tokarev pistol, while the Germans had the MP40 sub-machinegun, MP44 assault rifle and either P08 or P38 pistols. Meanwhile, a special banner party with 'Red Banner No. 5', given to the 150th Rifle Division by the Military Council of the 3rd Shock Army was despatched by Captain Stefan Neustroyev to find a way onto the roof. Eventually, two sergeants from the banner party under Lieutenant Berest managed to find their way to the back of the building and reach the roof via some stairs. Here they found a mounted statue and wedged the staff of the banner into a convenient crevice. This action was officially recorded at 22.50 and the two sergeants in question, M.A. Yegorov and M.V. Kantaria, received the award of Hero of the Soviet Union. The next day, photographs were taken to commemorate this event, but the photographer, Yevgeni Khaldei, found that the flag was too high and so changed places with the two men to produce the famous scene with the Red Flag having the background of the Brandenburg Gate, rather than the sky. (Peter Dennis)

through the buildings on the Schlieffenufer in order to attack the Kroll Opera House, in which the Germans had established a formidable strongpoint. The main attack towards the Reichstag was resumed at 11.30 and then again at 13.00, both attacks being pinned down with the help from the Zoo Flak Tower. At 14.25 MajGen Shatilov, commanding the 150th Rifle Division, reported that he had seen a red flag over the steps of the Reichstag, a message that quickly made its way up the chain of command, but when war correspondents made their way to the scene, they found the Soviet infantry still only halfway across Königsplatz. Painfully aware of the error, Shatilov ordered his troops to raise a flag whatever the cost. The attack was once again resumed at 18.00 and this time, with close support of armour and artillery, Soviet infantry managed to make it up the steps of the Reichstag and blast a small hole in the bricked up doorway. As more and more Soviet infantry entered, vicious hand-to-hand fighting spread throughout the floors of the building. Meanwhile, a special banner party with 'Red Banner No. 5' was despatched to find a way onto the roof. Eventually they did so, with the flag having been recorded as being raised at 22.50, some 70 minutes before May Day in Moscow.

Elsewhere, the 5th Shock Army's 26th Guards Rifle Corps continued to reduce the German strongpoint at the Börse S-Bahn Station, which was eventually taken, followed by an attack on the next strongpoint, the Telegraph Office. The 32nd Rifle Corps attacked across the Spree, towards the Schloss Berlin (the old Royal Palace), the Cathedral and the Reichsbank. The 2nd and 3rd Guards Tank Armies converged on the S-Bahn tracks that denoted the inter-front boundary, but the 2nd was having great difficulty in moving forward as its integral infantry had been greatly depleted.

A picture showing the devastation caused to the centre of the city with clouds of smoke rising from burning buildings as the garrison surrendered to the Red Army. Some of the barricades and obstacles thrown up by the Germans can be seen in the foreground. (Topfoto/Topham)

The remains of Busse's 9th Army finally made it to the village of Kummersdorf and briefly rested in the woods. They then broke through another Soviet cordon on the Berlin-Luckenwalde road and fought their way westwards, guided by Wenck's radio. The last remaining Tiger tank led the charge against the 5th Guards Mechanized Corps' positions and the survivors, utterly exhausted, reached the 12th Army's lines early the next morning.

At 15.20, Adolf Hitler and Eva Braun committed suicide in their sitting-room in the Führerbunker. Their bodies were taken out into the Chancellery garden, placed in a ditch, doused in petrol and then set alight. They were then buried in a shell-hole. This left Göbbels as Chancellor who now attempted to contact the Soviets with an eye to organizing a ceasefire and recognition for the new government, with General Bokov recording that an Obst Heinersdorf, ObstLt Seifert and Lt Seger, along with an Obergefreiter carrying a white flag approached the Soviet lines. They talked with Col V. S. Antonov of the 301st Rifle Division to arrange for Gen Krebs to negotiate with the Soviet High Command. They were sent back by Gen Berzarin after being told that Krebs would only be received when given authority to negotiate the German surrender.

1 MAY 1945

At midnight on 30 April, the battle for Berlin suddenly quietened down. It was May Day, and while both sides knew the end was close at hand, they reacted in different ways, the frontline Soviet troops becoming increasingly cautious as they did not want to be the last soldier to die in Berlin and the Germans taking the opportunity to rest and reorganize. Fighting and shelling continued sporadically, but in general it was only half-hearted and it was only where the Polish troops had been committed that there was there any real activity. Mohnke led Gen Krebs' party that included Weidling's Chief of Staff Obst von Dufving and Ostuf Neilands, who had changed his uniform to an Army Sonderführer, to the sector headquarters under ObstLt Seifert. They then proceeded to successfully cross Soviet lines and arrived at Chuikov's headquarters at 03.50. Krebs wanted recognition of the new Government and time to collect it, but the Soviets were only interested in unconditional surrender. It was agreed to set up a telephone line with Göbbels in the Führerbunker and after some initial confusion (where Waffen SS troops temporarily arrested von Dufving) two attempts were made to establish communications, but the line was cut both times. Krebs then returned with von Dufving and decided that the German response would have to be made in writing. Göbbels also sent a delegation of four officers to the command post of the 301st Rifle Division, 9th Rifle Corps. Col Antonov was instructed not to negotiate and instead storm the Chancellery. With both missions having failed, Göbbels then released the news of Hitler's death to Grossadmiral Dönitz, which the latter broadcast over Radio Hamburg, and opted for suicide along with his wife and six children.

During the morning, Spandau Citadel, an ancient fortress (complete with moat) dominating the town at the junction of the Spree and Havel, surrendered to the 47th Army having exacted a significant toll from the

2nd Guards Tank Army with aggressive patrolling and a staunch defence. Fighting continued within the Reichstag all day, with the German defence now under the command of Ostuf Babick of the SS 'Anhalt' Regiment, whose headquarters was located in a building across the street but connected to it via a tunnel. The building caught fire, adding to the misery of the combatants, and while the upper storeys were gradually cleared, the defence fought on from the cellars. The 5th Shock Army faced a difficult task in capturing the Ministry for Justice, the Foreign Office, the Air Ministry, the Reichs Main Security Office, the Reichs Chancellery and the Post Office Ministry. All were housed in enormous, well-constructed buildings and progress was slow, although it did manage to capture the Zeughaus (Armoury) and the State Library on the north side of the Unter-den-Linden, the State Opera and the Reichsbank to the south, as well as the Gestapo and Reichs Main Security Office on Prinz Albert Strasse. The 8th Guards Army had crossed Bellvuestrasse into Siegesallee, taken the Potsdamer Railway Station and was fighting for the Saarlandstrasse U-Bahn Station. The 2nd Guards Tank Army, having been reinforced by the 1st Polish Infantry Division, cleared the barricade on Kaiser-Friedrich-Strasse and took a church near Karl-August-Platz. It found it difficult to advance along the Landwehr Canal however, due to intense defensive fire, which, given the close-quarters nature of the terrain, made even JS-2 tanks vulnerable. The 3rd Guards Tank Army managed to make it across the Kurfürstendamm late in the day against fierce German opposition (mainly from surviving elements of the 'Müncheberg' Panzer Division) and eventually met up with the 2nd Guards Tank Army in Savignyplatz, to the southwest of the Tiergarten Flak Tower. With these developments, Weidling quickly came to the conclusion that surrender was the only viable option and so, after a discussion with the surviving members of the Berlin Defence Area command including Obst Wöhlermann, decided to enter into negotiations with the Soviets as soon as possible after midnight. There were, however, several breakout attempts during the night, a number of which succeeded.

The scene outside the Führerbunker. This pile of earth at the rear entrance to the underground shelter is reportedly where Adolf Hitler and Eva Braun were cremated after their suicide on 30 April 1945. Their bodies were then buried in a shell hole nearby. (Topfoto/Topham)

The Reichstag, shortly after the end of the battle, May 1945. In the foreground lays a wrecked German 8.8cm Flak 36/37 gun. This formidable weapon started life as an AA gun. It was soon found to be deadly against enemy tanks, however, and could fire a 10.4kg anti-tank shell over 17km. (Top foto/Novosti)

A photograph of a Soviet T-34/85 near the Brandenburg Gate. From the relaxed disposition of the crew and the soldiers picking their way through the debris nearer the monument, the photograph was probably taken after the fighting had finished. (From the fonds of the RGAKFD at Krasnogorsk)

The day also saw the linking up of the survivors of the Army Detachment 'Spree' and the 20th Panzergrenadier Division with Wenck's 12th Army who, along with Busse's 9th Army then promptly withdrew, closing the last corridor to the west. The German force negotiated their surrender to the US 9th Army under Gen Stimpson and managed to complete their crossing of the Elbe by 7 May 1945.

OPPOSITE The famous photograph by Yevgeny Khaldei showing Sergeants M. A. Yegorov and M. V. Kantaria as they raise Red Banner No. 5 above the Reichstag. This was a staged re-enactment as the actual flag-raising occurred just before 11 o'clock at night and it is clearly daylight in the photograph. (Topfoto/Topham)

2 MAY 1945

The next day saw the final assault on the Reichs Chancellery by the 9th Rifle Corps and, while the majority of the defenders had already withdrawn, some resistance was encountered. The building was quickly taken and Maj Anna Nikulina raised the Red Flag on the rooftop. Meanwhile, a German party under von Dufving had managed to make

The Red Flag goes up over the Reichstag . . . again. The Soviets reintroduced the carrying of battalion and regimental standards for the attack on Berlin. As it was essential to have propaganda photos of the event, enthusiastic flag-waving scenes occurred all over the roof. (From the fonds of the RGAKFD at Krasnogorsk)

A German officer (in the leather coat) with a number of troops nearby who are just taking a momentary break. Over 400,000 German soldiers were taken prisoner during the Berlin Operation, many of whom never returned from the Soviet Union and others not being released until the 1950s. (Nik Cornish Library)

Soviet soldiers celebrate victory in Berlin, May 1945. One of the soldiers, a member of a tank crew, waves a Red Flag. While the greatest proportion of casualties was suffered by the infantry, the Red Army also lost a large number of tank personnel in the operation. (Topfoto/Topham)

contact with a regimental command post of the 47th Guards Rifle Division, under Guards-Colonel Semchenko, and relayed Weidling's desire to surrender. The news reached Chuikov, who asked von Dufving to return to his commander to tell him his offer had been accepted. Weidling and his command staff would be expected to surrender at 06.00, while the troops would surrender at 07.00, honourable terms being guaranteed, Chuikov then ordering a ceasefire in his area. Weidling then accompanied two Soviet officers across the Landwehr Canal at around 05.00 (the officers were working on Moscow time and had arrived an hour early) and in Chuikov's headquarters (watched as well by Col-Gen Sokolovsky) composed his letter of surrender, which read:

> On the 30th April the Führer, to whom we had all sworn an oath of allegiance, forsook us by committing suicide. Faithful to the Führer, you German soldiers were prepared to continue the battle for Berlin even though your ammunition was running out and the general situation made further resistance senseless.
>
> I now order all resistance to end immediately. Every hour you go on fighting adds to the terrible suffering of the Berlin population and our wounded. In agreement with the High Command of the Soviet Forces, I call on you to stop fighting forthwith.
>
> Weidling, General of Artillery, Former Commander Berlin Defence Area.

This format was accepted by the Soviets and, although the fighting was to stop by 13.00, it was nearer 17.00 when the fighting came to an end in the city, including the Reichstag. The silence, as they say, was deafening. All

Soviet soldiers from the 1st Ukrainian Front and American soldiers from the 1st US Army sit on the banks of the River Elbe after their historic link up, near the town of Torgau, 25 April 1945. Having managed to get this far, and in one piece, must have been a great relief to all Allied troops. (IWM, OWIL64545)

that remained was to move the German prisoners-of-war away from the city and for the Soviets to take on the burden of ensuring vital supplies were continued (or restored) to the civil population. While this was done as quickly and as practically possible, it proved difficult for the Soviets to immediately bring their troops under control following the announcement of the surrender and while Soviet troops could on the one hand show great generosity and kindness, on the other, numerous atrocities continued to be visited on the German civilian population over the next few days. Abortion rates surged in the following months as up to 100,000 women were raped in Berlin. The Soviet High Command was well aware that some of their troops were out of control and that, even more shockingly, they had raped Soviet women after their release from Nazi labour camps.

With the surrender of the Berlin Garrison, Koniev was able to start withdrawing his 1st Ukrainian Front southwards to take part in the offensive (in conjunction with 2nd and 4th Ukrainian Fronts) against Army Group Centre in Czechoslovakia. Meanwhile, Rokossovsky's 2nd Byelorussian Front continued its operations north of Berlin and had reached a line linking Wittenberge, Parchim and Bad Doberan, while the British 21st Army Group had occupied the towns of Lübeck and Wismar and the US 9th Army had reached Ludwigslust and Schwerin. The Germans now found themselves squeezed into a very small pocket, now only some 15 to 20 miles across, and so von Manteuffel and von Tippelskirch decided to surrender their armies to the Americans. With the remainder of 1st Byelorussian Front (33rd Army, 69th Army, 3rd Army, 47th Army and 1st Polish Army) closing up to the River Elbe, except in the area held by Wenck's 12th Army, Operation *Berlin* came to an end.

The cost of the operation, and of Stalin's desire to get there before the Western Allies, was staggering. Between 16 April and 6 May, the Soviets

listed the three main fronts involved as capturing some 480,000 prisoners (with around 70,000 taken in Berlin), 1,500 tanks and self-propelled guns, 8,600 artillery pieces and 4,500 aircraft. Their own casualties are listed as 304,887 killed, wounded and missing, along with the loss of 2,156 tanks and self-propelled guns, 1,220 artillery pieces and 527 aircraft, although the true cost is likely to be higher. It is almost impossible to give an accurate figure of German military and civilian casualties within Berlin itself, due to the collapse of the civil administration towards the end of the battle, but it has been suggested that up to 22,000 civilians died from causes directly attributable to the battle and a similar number of military personnel, although many of these were accorded no military burial and just dumped in mass graves or buried in the trenches they died defending.

AFTERMATH

Two days after the Berlin Garrison had surrendered, at 18.20 on 4 May 1945, Gen E. Kinzel (GFM Busch's Chief of Staff) and Adm H. G. von Friedeburg (the new head of the Kriegsmarine) signed surrender documents relating to the German forces in the Netherlands, northwest Germany, the Friesian Islands, Heligoland and Schleswig-Holstein, at FM Montgomery's 21st Army Group headquarters on Lüneburg Heath. The same happened three days later, at 02.41 on 7 May 1945 at the Rheims school that housed SHAEF headquarters. GenObst Alfred Jodl (Chief of Staff, OKW), Adm Friedeburg and Maj Wilhelm Oxenius (Luftwaffe) signed the surrender document, along with LtGen Walter Bedell Smith (Eisenhower's Chief of Staff), LtGen Sir Frederick Morgan (for Great Britain), Gen Francois Sévez (for France) and MajGen Ivan Susloparov (for the Soviet Union). They were followed by LtGen Carl A. Spaatz, Vice-Adm Harold M. Burrough and Air Mshl J. M. Robb signing for the US Army Air Force, the Royal Navy and RAF respectively. The next day saw Air Chf Mshl Sir Arthur Tedder, along with LtGen Spaatz flying to Berlin for the final act of surrender. The ceremony took place at 1st Byelorussian Front's headquarters. GFM Wilhelm Keitel (Head of the OKW and Hitler's Chief of Staff), Adm Friedeburg (Kriegsmarine) and General Stumpff (Luftwaffe) appeared before Marshal Zhukov, Gen de Lattre de Tassigny, Tedder and Spaatz. All had signed the surrender documents by 00.28. With the unconditional surrender of Nazi Germany, the European part of the Second World War would end at 23.01, 8 May 1945.

GenObst Alfred Jodl, Adm Friedeburg and Maj Wilhelm Oxenius signing the documents of unconditional surrender in Rheims, at the Supreme Headquarters Allied Expeditionary Force, 7 May 1945. Even though there were only a few days between each of the signings, this time allowed hundreds of thousands of German soldiers and civilians to escape west. (Topfoto)

A picture showing Soviet soldiers distributing food to the city's residents. Soviet troops could show both great kindness and generosity or commit crimes ranging from looting to rape. While the Soviet High Command tried to bring their troops under control as quickly as possible, many sought revenge for what the Nazis had done in Mother Russia. (Topfoto/Novosti)

Although the time between the various signings was short, hundreds of thousands of German troops managed to make their way west to surrender to the Western Allies, and the Kriegsmarine evacuated its Baltic positions. The Allied armies had exercised their 'right of pursuit' and followed the retreating German forces well past the demarcation line as set out in the Yalta Agreement, Montgomery by about 45 miles and Bradley by about 125 miles. The day after the signing of the official surrenders, Stalin insisted on the implementation of the undertakings given at Yalta. Had he kept his own promises, though? Clearly the Soviet NKVD were in the process of eliminating any possible opposition to the setting up of Communist regimes in Eastern Europe, particularly in respect of Poland, where the commission set up in the Kremlin after Yalta to oversee the reorganization of the Government was paralysed by Molotov's obstruction. In these circumstances, Churchill wrote on 4 June to the new US President, Harry Truman, indicating that the retreat of the Western Allied armies to their demarcation lines should not be undertaken without having a number of these outstanding issues between the Great Powers resolved. The behaviour of the Soviet occupation authorities in Austria and the interference with the missions of the Western Powers caused Churchill to write again on 9 June. Truman ignored these arguments and decided that the US Army would start withdrawing on 21 June while the military chiefs would sort out the quadripartite occupation of Berlin and the access to it by road, rail and air. On 15 July 1945 just before the Potsdam conference began, the Red Army had already taken up its advanced positions 30 miles from the centre of Hamburg, within artillery range of Kassel and less than 80 miles from Mainz on the Rhine. Churchill wrote, 'It was a fateful decision'.

The city was split into zones of occupation, along the same lines as Germany itself, with the Soviet zone in the east and the Americans, British and French each having a zone in the western part of the city. American forces reached Berlin on 1 July, while the British arrived the next day. The French did in fact initially enter Berlin without a zone of occupation, with both the Americans and Soviets steadfastly refusing to concede any territory. It was left to the British to break the deadlock and donate two of

A photograph taken by Sergeant Hewitt showing Sergeant R. S. Baker of the Army Film and Photographic Unit standing in the centre courtyard of the ruined Reichs Chancellery in Berlin, 2 July 1945. After the war, the Soviets used the red marble that had decorated large areas of the interior to refurbish parts of East Berlin. (IWM, BU8569)

their boroughs in northwest Berlin to create the French sector. With reconstruction proceeding apace, the four military governors presented the city authorities with a draft constitution that was to be adopted following elections in the autumn. The elections proved to be a bitter setback for the Communists (who only got 20 per cent of the vote), despite such tricks as handing out free food, shoes and cigarettes in the Soviet sector, free fruit and vegetables in the western sectors and occasionally turning off the electricity to demonstrate their power.

The tensions that were gradually affecting relations between the Western Allies and Soviet Union also impacted upon Germany and Berlin. The American initiative, called the Marshal Plan, designed to stimulate economic and political recovery in Europe, was meeting strong Soviet resistance and so in February 1948 the Western Allies agreed to combine their zones into a single economic and politically democratic unit. This decision so enraged the Soviets that they walked out of the Allied Control Council (for Germany as a whole) on 20 March without setting a date for the next, followed by Berlin's Kommandatura (the Allied Military Council for Berlin) on 16 June. The Soviets then began to interfere with Allied road and rail traffic going to and from the city. A Vickers Viking from British European Airways crashed after it had been buzzed by a Soviet Yak-3 fighter that collided with it while turning for a second pass. The Soviets finally cut the land routes to the city on 24 June. The Western Allies took the decision to airlift the necessary supplies for Berlin's survival in to the three airfields at Gatow, Tegal and Tempelhof, using three narrow air corridors from West Germany. The aircraft used initially consisted of C-47 Dakotas but were soon augmented by American C-54 Skymasters and British Avro Yorks and thus the tonnage delivered rapidly increased from 1,400 to 5,500 by January 1949. The Soviets finally lifted the blockade in May, due to both the unfavourable international reaction and the Allied counter-blockade, but the airlift went on until

September. The human and material cost had been substantial with some

Prime Minister Winston Churchill being shown the ruins of the Reichstag during his tour of Berlin, 16 July 1945. Photograph by Capt W. Lockeyear. With the end of the war in Europe, Churchill had forseen the Cold War and warned Truman not to withdraw American troops until differences with the Soviets had been resolved. (IWM, BU8949)

The scene in front of the Brandenburg Gate on 13 August 1961. As a large crowd of West Berliners gathers in the square opposite, East German soldiers and militia put up barbed wire and barricades, which were to form the basis of the Berlin Wall. (Topfoto/Topham)

70 aircrew and seven Germans being killed as the Soviets often staged mock air attacks - the weather was often very difficult, pilots were tired and coal dust would work its way into controls. However, the West had demonstrated its resolve in the face of Soviet pressure.

As the tensions between East and West gradually developed into the Cold War, Berlin became a central point in the confrontation as East and West conducted a covert intelligence war across the city. The Federal Republic of Germany came into being in 1949, followed by the German Democratic Republic. In June 1953, a call by the East German Government (that had been established in East Berlin) for a doubling of effort with no increase in wages brought about a strike across the country. Thousands of workers marched on the Ministries building (the old Air Ministry under Goring) demanding the Government resign and

ABOVE **A dead German soldier (in this instance, a Reichsarbeitdienst labour corpsman) lays near the Brandenburg Gate. But was he a victim of friend or foe? Flying courts martial manned by fanatical SS officers were as much a threat to the German defenders as the Soviets were. (From the fonds of the RGAKFD at Krasnogorsk)**

ABOVE, LEFT **A photograph showing a party of women forming a chain gang to clear rubble from damaged buildings. Large areas had been devastated by the end of the war, not only by the ground-fighting but by the Allied bombing campaign that had started in earnest in 1943. Taken by Sergeant Hewitt on 7 July 1945. (IWM, BU8684)**

free elections, which in turn provoked Soviet intervention. The uprising was crushed with several hundred protesters and police being killed. Berlin also saw the creation of one of the strongest and lasting symbols of the Cold War. In an effort to stop the drain of skilled workers from East Germany (over two million since 1949), the leader of the GDR, Walter Ulbricht, set up barricades along the Soviet sector's 30-mile border on 12 August 1961, to seal East Berlin off from the West. The action sparked off a major crisis between East and West but over time, the barbed wire and barricade wall gradually made way to bricks, mortar and concrete. There were many attempts to cross the wall, many succeeding, but a number ended in tragedy. This was followed by a visit from President John F. Kennedy in June 1963 and the signing of the Quadripartite Agreement in September 1971 that saw the Western Allies officially recognize the GDR in return for better contacts between the two Germanys. With the arrival of Gorbachev's Perestroika and Glasnost, relations between East and West quickly improved until the point came whereby the Eastern Bloc imploded in a relatively bloodless revolution during the winter of 1989–90. By October 1990, Germany had once again become a unified country and the decision was taken in June 1991 that Berlin would once again become the capital of a united Germany. The German Parliament would move from Bonn and return to its old seat of power, the Reichstag, which was renovated between 1995 and 1999 by the British architect Sir Norman Foster.

THE BATTLEFIELD TODAY

Berlin today is a large, prosperous city having an area of just under 900 square kilometres and a population of around 3.4 million. The city was restored as the country's capital in 1999 when the German Bundestag (Parliament) moved from Bonn to its new home in the refurbished Reichstag. Despite the euphoria of unification, the joining of East and West Germany (indeed, East and West Berlin) has not been without its problems, and, while the Federal Republic has struggled under the cost of financing the economic, financial and industrial recovery of the east, modernization has not been as rapid as many would have liked. This has led to the growth of extreme right-wing political elements (particularly in the east) who have directed their anger at foreigners, mainly Turkish workers, who have been the target of a number of racist attacks.

Berlin sits in the middle of an area known from medieval times as the Mark of Brandenburg, now called the Bundesland (Federal State) of Brandenburg. In 2001, the 23 administrative districts were reduced to 12 in an effort to reduce bureaucracy, but many of the old district names continue to be used. In the middle of the city lies the brooding and monstrous Fernsehturm (TV Tower), a useful orientation point visible from most of central Berlin. The Unter den Linden, the fashionable avenue of aristocratic old Berlin, extends from the Brandenburg Gate to Alexanderplatz, once the heart of the German Democratic Republic. Some of Berlin's finest museums are on Museumsinsel in the Spree, the original centre of the metropolis. West of the Brandenburg Gate, the boulevard runs through Tiergarten, a huge landscaped park. The

A Soviet victory parade outside the ruins of the Reichstag, summer 1945. Stalin's desire to get to Berlin before the Western Allies for political and strategic reasons ultimately cost the Red Army over 300,000 casualties and over 2,000 destroyed tanks in more than 17 days of bitter fighting. (Topfoto/Novosti)

Victory Column at its centre appeared in the Wim Wender's film *Wings of Desire* (1987). The commercial centre of West Berlin glitters just to the south. The real revelation for visitors at the moment, however, is Friedrichshain, once a grotty district favoured by backpackers for its cheapness and site of one of the massive flak towers. Things are still cheap here by Berlin standards, but the area south of Frankfurter Allee has suddenly become popular for its nightlife, with new bars and clubs popping up everywhere. South of the Brandenburg Gate, in areas once occupied by the Wall, Berlin's newest quarter has emerged around the Potsdamer Platz. During the 1990s this area underwent massive redevelopment under the architects Wilmer and Sattler and now contains a number of landmark towers, a shopping arcade, an entertainment centre and residential buildings.

There are, however, a few major remnants of the Third Reich and the battle for Berlin that have survived. The first is a still intact wing of Joseph Göbbels' Propaganda Ministry, just along the Mohrenstrasse, in what used to be called Wilhelm Platz, from where he also controlled the Reichskulturkammer, the governmental department that controlled the arts. South along Wilhelmstrasse, which happened to be the heart of the Third Reich, stands the former Reichs Air Ministry, a harsh, unadorned structure which has become a finance and tax building. On one side is a mural to the socialist ideal of the workers paradise, a picture that is doubly ironic in that it replaced the almost identical National Socialist mural, and acted as a rallying point to the workers who were striking during the 1953 uprising. Further south along Niederkirchnerstrasse, which is in fact the renamed Prinz Albrechtstrasse, after a female Soviet spy who was executed by the Germans at Ravensbrück, lies the site of a former art school that was taken over by the Gestapo and

Sicherheitsdienst to become their headquarters, the most chilling address in Berlin. The Gestapo eventually outgrew No. 8 Prinz Albrechtstrasse and took over parts of a number of other buildings in the district, the whole complex becoming known as Prinz Albrecht Terrain. There is now a museum called the 'Topography of Terror' that displays exhibits and photos from this terrible era to remind people of just what happened here.

Finally, there are the Brandenburg Gate, the site of the Reichs Chancellery (Reichskanzlei) and Führerbunker, as well as the Reichstag. The Brandenburg Gate has been refurbished and was unveiled by Bill Clinton in October 2002. The Chancellery had its red marble stripped from its walls by the Soviets after the Second World War to help rebuild parts of Berlin and construct their War Memorial over in Treptower Park. Some 5,000 soldiers are buried at the site, a fraction of those who lost their lives in the battle. The building was then demolished. It was here that Hitler had his bunker, located some 50 feet below ground, although it has now been sealed. The Reichstag was renovated by Sir Norman Foster between 1995 and 1999 and still contains many walls that have the graffiti scrawled on them by Soviet soldiers. Other sites of interest include the grave of Marlene Dietrich in Friednau Cemetery, the Plötzensee Memorial to the thousands who died in the prison there, the Berlin Wall Memorial on Bernauer Strasse, the Checkpoint Charlie Museum at the corner of Kochstrasse and Friedrichstrasse, and the People's Court, which is now the Berlin Constitutional Court in the Kammergericht (Chambers of Justice) on Elssholzstrasse.

As far as the Seelow Heights are concerned, the area is much as it was back in 1945 although improvements in the drainage system means there is much less swampland in evidence. There is a T-34/85 erected on a plinth in the centre of Kienitz by the GDR Government with a plaque that reads: '31 January 1945 – Kienitz, the first place in our country to have been liberated from fascism. Glory and honour to the fighting soldiers to the 5th Shock and 2nd Guards Tank Army'. A memorial to the battle for the Seelow Heights lies in Seelow itself, along with the graves of those Soviet soldiers who were awarded the hero of the Soviet Union, but the main Soviet cemetery lies at the foot of the Reitwein Spur that was also used by Zhukov as the site of his command post. Smaller cemeteries are scattered all across the area, often in the villages and towns, and are well tended today, such as the ones in Sachsendorf and Letschin.

BIBLIOGRAPHY AND FURTHER READING

Altner, H., *Berlin – Dance of Death*, Spellmount, Staplehurst (2002)

Bauer, E., (LtCol) *The History of World War Two*, Orbis Publishing, London (1979)

Beevor, A., *Berlin – The Downfall 1945*, Viking / Penguin, London, 2002. See also the book's webpage, addressed http://www.antonybeevor.com/Berlin/berlinmenu.htm, for additional information.

Bell, K., 'Bloody Battle for Berlin' in *World War II*, March 1998, Volume 12, Issue 7, pp.22–29.

Clark, A., *Barbarossa: The Russian–German Conflict 1941–1945*, Cassell & Co, London (2001)

Erickson, J., *The Road to Berlin*, Cassell & Co, London (2003)

Gunter, G., *Last Laurels: The German Defence of Upper Silesia, January–May 1945*, Helion & Company, Solihull (2002)

Hastings, M., *Armageddon: The Battle for Germany 1944–45*, Macmillan, London (2004)

Hirschbiegel, O. (Dir), *Downfall*, Historical Drama, Constantin Films, 155 minutes (2005). Official site: http://www.downfallthefilm.com/.

Holmes, R. (ed.), *The Oxford Companion to Military History*, Oxford University Press, Oxford (2001)

Joachimsthaler, A., *The Last Days of Hitler: Legend, Evidence and Truth*, Cassell & Co, London (2000)

Jukes, G., *The Second World War (5): The Eastern Front 1941–1945*, Osprey Publishing, Oxford (2002), Essential History Series No. 24

Keegan, J., 'Berlin' in *Military History Quarterly* (Winter 1998), pp.72–83

Le Tissier, T., *Berlin – Then and Now*, Battle of Britain Prints International Ltd, London (1992)

Le Tissier, T., *Race for the Reichstag – The 1945 Battle for Berlin*, Frank Cass, London (1999)

Le Tissier, T., *The Battle of Berlin 1945*, Jonathan Cape, London (1988)

Le Tissier, T., *With our Backs to Berlin – The German Army in Retreat 1945*, Sutton Publishing, Stroud (1999)

Le Tissier, T., *Zhukov at the Oder – The Decisive Battle for Berlin*, Praeger, Westport, CT, (1996)

Lucas, J., *Last Days of the Reich*, Grafton Books, London (1987)

Orlov, A., 'The Price of Victory, The Cost of Aggression' in *History Today* (April 2005), pp. 24–26

Read, A. & Fisher, D., *The Fall of Berlin*, Hutchinson, London (1992)

Remme, Tilman, 'The Battle for Berlin', part of the BBC History Website, located at http://www.bbc.co.uk/cgi-bin/history, as of 16/02/2003

Ryan, C., *The Last Battle*, Touchstone, New York (1995)

Strawson, J., *The Battle for Berlin*, Batsford, London (1974)

Thomas, N., *The German Army 1939–45 (4): Eastern Front 1943–45*, Osprey Publishing, Oxford (1999), Men-at-Arms Series No. 330

Toland, J., *The Last 100 Days*, Phoenix, London (1996)

Williamson, G., *The Waffen SS (3): 11. to 23. Divisions*, Osprey Publishing, Oxford (2004), Men-at-Arms Series No. 415

Zaloga, S., *Bagration 1944*, Osprey Publishing, Oxford (1996), Campaign Series No. 42.

Zaloga, S., *The Red Army of the Great Patriotic War 1941–5*, Osprey Publishing, Oxford (1984), Men-at-Arms Series No. 216

Ziemke, Earl F., *Battle for Berlin: End of the Third Reich*, MacDonald & Co, London (1969), Purnell's History of the Second World War Battle Book No. 6

Ziemke, Earl F., *Stalingrad to Berlin: The German Defeat in the East*, Dorset Press / Center for Military History, Washington DC (1968)

INDEX

Figures in **bold** refer to illustrations